Meeting
Friend & Stranger

Fostering respect and mutual understanding
between the religions

---

*I truly understand that God shows no partiality,
but in every nation anyone who fears him
and does what is right is acceptable to him (Acts 10:35)*

A teaching document of the
Catholic Bishops' Conference of England and Wales

Meeting God in Friend and Stranger

Catholic Bishops' Conference of England and Wales

Published by The Catholic Truth Society.

The Catholic Truth Society
40-46 Harleyford Road
London
SE11 5AY
www.cts-online.org.uk

Cover image: *Cityscape of Jerusalem through a window of a church* © iStockphoto.com

ISBN 978 1 86082 663 4

To the memory of
Bishop Charles Henderson
and
Mrs Ann Noonan

Contents

Foreword

In Britain today we are engaged in a process of learning how to construct and live in a society made up of people of many different faiths. This is a process from which no-one is excused. Our common good depends on it.

I am very pleased to introduce this Teaching Document of the Bishops' Conference of England and Wales: *Meeting God in Friend and Stranger.*

Two important convictions lie behind this document.

The first is that belief in God, as expressed in the great religious traditions of humanity, is a force for good in our society today. There are those who would have us believe that this is not so, who insist that religious beliefs are divisive and, at worst, belittling. Yet the quest for God is rooted in the spirit of every human being and brings with it the quest for holiness, goodness, compassion, forgiveness, perseverance, humility and truth. Of course, the history of this quest is marked with failure and sin. But so are all of our strivings. The religious quest, properly understood, tackles these failings head on, proclaiming the need for every person to turn away from corruption, selfishness and the misuse of power in the effort to know the mystery of God and the mystery of our common humanity.

The second conviction is that the Catholic faith instructs us and guides us not only in the unique pathway to God through Jesus Christ, but also in the manner in which we are to learn about and cooperate with people of other faiths.

This aspect of Catholic teaching is fully and faithfully presented in this document. It is, in the first place, for members of the Catholic Church. Yet I am sure that many other people, those who are followers of other religions and those who do not claim a religious allegiance, will also find guidance and insight here.

I am confident, therefore, that this document is an important contribution to the task of dialogue within our society, a task and a duty which falls to us all.

+Vincent Nichols

Most Reverend Vincent Nichols

Archbishop of Westminster

President, Catholic Bishops' Conference of England and Wales

PREFACE

From one ancestor he made all nations to inhabit the whole earth, and he allotted the times of their existence and the boundaries of the places where they would live, so that they would search for God and perhaps grope for him and find him – though indeed he is not far from each one of us. (Ac 17:26-27)

For a great many people in the world their religious allegiance claims their deepest feelings and loyalties. As a consequence, any activity that promotes respect and better understanding among believers must contribute to peace, at a time when justice and peace are so threatened.

We are very conscious nowadays of the smallness of our world, and of how the potential for both understanding and conflict have increased. Today's means of communication together with increased migration have brought religions and cultures in closer contact than ever before, so that our society in Britain has become in many places multi-cultural and multi-religious.

The Catholic bishops of England and Wales, therefore, think it opportune to address Catholics on this matter, and to encourage them to look upon dialogue as an essential, though certainly not an easy, part of their witness in Britain today.

The challenge is a real one. Clergy and laity have many calls on their time and energy, and the smaller their number the less time and energy they have to meet the challenge. Dialogue with believers of other religions is a new concept for many Catholics, and they may well feel that it is 'one challenge too far'. Some will ask how it can be reconciled with Our Lord's missionary call to *proclaim the good news to every creature (Mk* 16:15). Others will point out that for members of some other religions there is a similar difficulty: is not dialogue, as a careful listening to another belief, a denial of one's own?

We recognise these difficulties, but we are still convinced that to seek dialogue is the way forward for the Church of our time. Our conviction stems from the need to promote world peace, as Pope Benedict XVI has often said, but it also stems from the fact that the Church is called by Christ to be, like himself, the humble servant of God and of our fellow men and women. The Second Vatican Council described the Church as the 'sacrament' or sign and instrument of communion with God and one another in our divided world[1], the world that God created and that he loved so much that he gave his only Son as its Saviour (*Jn* 3:16).

Working ecumenically: This is a teaching document of the bishops of the Catholic Church in England and Wales and is naturally addressed to the Catholic community. But dialogue with other world religions is often something we conduct 'ecumenically', that is, jointly with our fellow Christians.[2] We would therefore like to offer this to our ecumenical partners within the Christian family, to clarify where the Catholic Church stands in this matter and as a way of fostering the cooperation between us. We have much to learn from one another.[3]

Dialogue with our Culture: It is important to relate this document to another conversation that is taking place, between the Church and the general culture of our time. We draw attention to *On the Way to Life: Promoting and Supporting Catholic Education in England and Wales* (2005), which is an analysis of our culture, focussing especially on the nature of secularism, and seeks to put forward a vision of Catholic modernity.[4]

---

[1] Second Vatican Council, Dogmatic Constitution on the Church *Lumen Gentium* (*Light of the Nations*). Titles of Vatican documents are traditionally taken from the opening Latin words.

[2] The word 'ecumenical' refers to dialogue between Christians, with the aim of restoring unity in Christ in one visible Church, whereas 'interreligious dialogue' refers to that between the various religions of the world. The aim is not complete unity in one body, but a growth in respect and understanding for the purpose of peace and the growth of the Kingdom of God.

[3] We would like to mention here a production of the Mission and Public Affairs Council of the Church of England entitled *Presence and Engagement* (2005), which explores the Church of England's situation in our multi-religious society.

[4] Published by the Catholic Education Service, *On the Way to Life* is a study by the Heythrop Institute for Religion, Ethics and Public Life commissioned by the Bishops' Conference. The document provided a starting point for a process of reflection which is ongoing.

There are forces of secularism in our society, and this affects all religions, yet religion still remains a vital force within it. This is now acknowledged by government, and we hope that what we offer here may be of service to the wider community as a way of overcoming divisions and fostering social harmony.

The use of the word 'Church' in this document: The word 'Church' in Catholic belief and usage can, of course, refer to a church building – a building 'belonging to the Lord', but more fundamentally it refers to the People 'gathered together' by the Lord, the 'People of God'. As the Second Vatican Council emphasised in its documents on the Church and on Ecumenism,[5] Christ founded one Church, and one Church only, the people gathered together by the risen Christ through the power of the Holy Spirit: *There is one body and one Spirit, just as you were called to the one hope of your calling: one Lord, one faith, one baptism (Ep* 4:4-5). It is Catholic belief that this one Church has continued to exist, and will continue to exist, in all essentials, in spite of the wounds of human sin, in the Catholic Church – that is, in the community that is in union with the bishops who are in visible communion with the Bishop of Rome.

However, it is also Catholic belief that all baptised Christians, in their various communities and traditions at present institutionally separate from the Catholic Church, are in spite of that united in various degrees of communion with the Catholic Church. As the Decree on Ecumenism puts it, *all who have been justified by faith in baptism are incorporated into Christ, and therefore have the right to be called Christian, and with good reason are accepted as brothers and sisters by the children of the Catholic Church (UR* 5).

The word 'Church', therefore, can vary in its meaning, and inevitably it varies in this document. Normally it refers to the Catholic Church but the meaning should be clear from the context in which it is used.

---

[5] See LG 8; *Unitatis Redintegratio* 1-5.

The Authority of this Teaching Document: This text has been approved unanimously by all the bishops of England and Wales. Because of the responsibility we share of leading the Catholic faithful of our two nations, we wish to give guidance on living our Catholic life in the multi-religious society that is ours. The degree of authority to be acknowledged in the different parts of the document will vary: those in the first place to the authority of revealed truth recorded and interpreted in the Scriptures; there is the teaching of the Second Vatican Council and the Popes; there is that of the departments (known as Dicasteries) of the Holy See, especially the Pontifical Council for Interreligious Dialogue; and there is the authority embodied in the agreed decisions of all the bishops of England and Wales concerning matters where we have rightful pastoral responsibility.

Chapter 1: WHAT IS 'INTERRELIGIOUS DIALOGUE'?

Indeed, the whole history of man's salvation is one long, varied dialogue, which marvellously begins with God and which he prolongs with men in so many different ways.[6]

1. In common parlance the word 'dialogue' usually means a conversation in words, but in the Church's teaching interreligious dialogue means far more than that. In 1984 the Holy See's Dicastery for dialogue with other religions described it in this way:

> *[Dialogue]... means not only discussion, but also includes all positive and constructive interreligious relations with individuals and communities of other faiths which are directed at mutual understanding and enrichment.*[7]

2. In an address to the Pontifical Council for Interreligious Dialogue in 1990 Pope John Paul II described it even more briefly:

> *Dialogue is not so much an idea to be studied as a way of living in positive relationship with others.*[8]

3. Interreligious dialogue, then, as the Catholic Church understands it, includes simply living as good neighbours with those of other religions, or working together in matters of common concern, such as in issues of justice, peace, the integrity of creation and so forth. It includes a willingness, according to circumstances, to try to understand better the religion of one's neighbours, and to experience something of their religious life and culture. In other words, dialogue is above all a frame of mind, an attitude.

---

[6] Pope Paul VI, Encyclical Letter *Ecclesiam Suam* (*His Church*) 1970, 70 (*See below*, n. 90).

[7] Secretariat for Non-Christians, *Reflections and Orientations on Dialogue and Mission* 1984, 3. The name of the Secretariat was later changed to the Pontifical Council for Interreligious Dialogue (PCID).

[8] Address to PCID, 26th April 1990. See Gioia, F., (ed.), *Interreligious Dialogue: the Official Teaching of the Catholic Church 1963-1995*, Pauline Books, 1997, p.431.

4. Another, more 'in depth' form of dialogue would be an actual conversation specifically about spiritual, theological or scholarly matters.

The 'Challenge of Difference'

5. In interreligious dialogue we converse, or relate in some other way, with those whose beliefs and values are, at least in part, different from our own. We try to cross the 'gulf of difference', and to be open to the truth and the goodness we might find there, however strange their expression might seem to us. In dialogue we can discover to what extent our teachings and values overlap, and where there are real differences. When there are such differences God may sometimes lead us into further truth about himself, because God's mystery can never be fully within our grasp, and the journey into it is endless. We are always learners, on a pilgrimage towards a greater fullness of truth. Sometimes, however, in the light of God's revelation in Christ, we may have to confess that what we are meeting is simply false, and not a glimpse of God's truth or holiness. It is an essential part of dialogue that, in courtesy, we say so.

6. Those we seek to have dialogue with vary considerably. Their concerns and their self-understanding will often challenge our expectations. Some groups or individuals may not want to collaborate at all, because of objections rooted in their religious or cultural traditions, or because of suspicion or fear. The notion of dialogue, especially in the strictest sense of a conversation where both sides are open to listening and being changed by learning and self-correction, and not merely as a form of bargaining, or of arguing and seeking to persuade, can be an utterly alien one. Sometimes those who do take part in dialogue will be criticised by their co-religionists. Those criticisms often issue from a defective or superficial understanding of the nature of dialogue itself.

7. It is useless to come to dialogue full of presuppositions about the other person or community, already convinced (consciously or not) that we know what they believe and how they behave. As far as we can we have to free ourselves of these premature judgments, 'empty

ourselves' so to speak, so that the other's real identity can be disclosed to us and we meet the real person and his or her real beliefs, and not some product of our imagination. We must certainly enter dialogue prepared to be surprised and to change our minds. Love of our neighbour, humility, and a respect for the dignity of the other person made in God's image demand that we do this – or at least try our best to do it. This is the only way of learning the true nature of another's beliefs and concerns.

8. We must realise too that the other person will have his or her share of preconceptions about us. We have to listen to these, and with patience make clear what we believe and what our values really are. We have to listen attentively, and speak honestly, in the spirit of Christ, the spirit of love of our neighbour. For a Christian, interreligious dialogue is a profoundly Christ-like work.

9. *Conclusion:* The challenge of difference, the task of meeting the followers of another religion in true dialogue, is the demanding one of combining genuine love and respect, and openness to unexpected truth and goodness, with a firm grasp of our own Christian faith and a readiness to be led by its light. The Catholic Church today, as we shall explain, recognises the presence of what is true and holy in other religions as being 'rays of the Truth' and 'seeds of the Word'; but the Church is also cautious about identifying those 'rays' and those 'seeds' too hastily. This caution should mark our dialogue, not to undermine it but to ensure its integrity.

Chapter 2:
THE CHANGING FACE OF BRITAIN

10. In many parts of Britain today Catholics will be living and working, not only alongside their fellow Christians and members of the Jewish Community, together with those of no religious belief, but also with followers of many other world religions.

11. The 2001 Census was the first to ask a question about people's religion. These statistics are by now somewhat out of date, but in round figures this was what emerged:[9]

41 million described themselves as Christian (72% of the population); 1.6 million as Muslim (3%), 558,000 as Hindu (1%), 336,000 as Sikh (0.6%), 267,000 as Jewish (0.5%), 149,000 as Buddhist (0.3%), 159,000 as members of other religions (0.3%), 8.6 million as of no religion (15%). 4.4 million (8%) did not say.

12. As with Christianity, most of these religions break down into numerous smaller groupings, based on confessional or ethnic factors.

13. The 'visibility' of other world religions has increased over the years. In many parts of the country mosques, gurdwaras and temples are a familiar sight, alongside churches and synagogues, all witnessing to the religious, cultural and ethnic identity of those who worship there.

14. Members of these communities have also grown in self-confidence as fellow citizens. They will be more ready to press for provision for their religious needs, and to object to behaviour they regard as offensive. At the same time they have had to adapt to the very different circumstances of modern British society concerning their traditional forms of worship and codes of conduct, and to the importance, or lack of importance, society attaches to these things. This can feel, at least to some, like a challenge to customs which are dear to them, and which they regard as central to their lives and religion.

---

[9] Office for National Statistics, Census, April 2001.

The Impact of World Events

15. We often hear talk of 'globalisation'. This refers to the process by which organisations, especially in the world of business, begin to operate on a global scale. The 'global village' is the whole world thought of as a single community, linked by the media and by all the means of communication that are available. We are almost instantly informed about events in other parts of the world, however distant, just as in former times news would travel rapidly from one end of a village to the other.

16. These events, at home as well as abroad, and the way they are reported, shape our attitudes towards people of other religions and cultures, and especially towards those living here in Britain. They also affect the newer communities themselves, and the relations between them.

17. Sometimes this global awareness, in all its immediacy, can have a beneficial effect, making us realise instinctively the unity of all human beings whatever their race or religion. The devastating tsunami of 26th December 2004 led to a world-wide outburst of generosity towards the victims and reminded us all of our solidarity with them. The earthquake in Pakistan in October 2005 also provoked a global response. The threat of climate change is by definition a global one, only effectively met by increased cooperation.

18. Tragically, other events have had the opposite effect. The attack on the United States in September 2001 and the subsequent military action in Afghanistan together with the intervention in Iraq beginning in 2003, have affected attitudes towards Muslims in Britain, and their attitude towards the rest of the population. These events have also influenced feelings towards immigrants and refugees from Muslim majority countries; they have reinforced prejudices and encouraged stereotyping. Innocent people have been victimised because of their appearance, or their ethnic or religious background. Sikhs have been attacked because of the actions of Al Qaeda-linked terrorists, and refugees from Afghanistan or Iraq have been targeted because of the actions of those from whom they were fleeing. Another example is the increase of anti-Semitism in the U.K. over the past few years, as a recent Parliamentary Report shows.[10]

The Position of Christianity

19. Church attendance has been falling in most Christian communities for some time now. The predominant secular culture looks on religious belief and practice as a private matter. Great weight is put on personal choice, and many are unwilling to commit themselves to any organised form of Christianity, and to any authority structure it might contain. Christianity no longer has the public status it once had. Yet the 2001 Census shows that over 70% of the population still wishes to identify itself as 'Christian', whatever meaning an individual might attach to that.

20. *The Catholic Community:* Fifty years ago Catholics in Britain were still a community clearly distinct from the rest of the population. This was partly because of a long history of anti-Catholic prejudice, and in earlier times persecution, but also because from the mid-nineteenth century onwards the majority of Catholics were immigrants, or immediately descended from immigrants, conscious of their different culture and identity. In addition, after the Catholic-Protestant division of Europe at the Reformation the Catholic Church was anxious to safeguard the Catholic faith of its members by forms of separation (in education, for example) from the institutions of the rest of British society. Nowadays the situation has changed: Catholics in England and Wales have become much more assimilated into mainstream culture.

21. The world-wide Catholic Church is itself a multi-racial community, having a rich diversity of its own. Nowadays the Catholic Church in England and Wales is a reflection of this, embracing the cultural diversity that is so much a feature of Catholicism across the world. Our parishes often include Catholics from Africa, India, Vietnam, South America, the Caribbean and the Philippines, not to mention those who came from Poland and Italy in the 1940s, and the immigrants from Eastern Europe over the past few years.

---

[10] Report of the All-Parliamentary Inquiry into Antisemitism, 2006.

22. The document of the Holy See *Erga Migrantes*[11] points out that this serves to heighten our awareness of what it means for the Church to be 'catholic', embracing all peoples. The Church's life in this country has been greatly enriched by this diversity, showing us how the one Gospel can be 'inculturated' in many different ways. Catholics, of all people, should respect diversity, not only the diversity among Catholics and Christians in general, but the diversity within the general population of other ethnic groups and religions. Of course immigration must be administered with care for the sake of the common good, but to resent diversity in principle is to exclude ourselves from the possibility of being enriched by what others might have to offer. This does not correspond to a Christian, and especially a Catholic, vision.

The Challenge of Pluralism

23. The word 'pluralism' has more than one meaning, but in today's use it can mean the same as 'plurality' or 'diversity': the co-existence in one society of many cultures, religions, philosophies and outlooks on life. In this sense of the word the Catholic Church does not only recognise pluralism as a fact but also respects it, in the sense that it supports everyone's right to freedom from persecution and prejudice, to an equal civil status within society, and to liberty and self-fulfilment within the constraints of the common good. Catholics should promote respect for this pluralism, so as to foster the legitimate rights and aspirations of their neighbours of other religions.

24. Within a democratic society this kind of pluralism is the basis necessary for dialogue, but it is also one of the beneficial results of dialogue. Dialogue helps us appreciate the gifts of the dialogue-partner's religion and culture more deeply and what these can contribute to the good of all.

25. *'Relativism':* The Catholic Church's attitude is in marked contrast to the 'relativist' understanding, which is such a common response to the religious pluralism we experience in Britain today. The relativist

---

[11] Pontifical Council for Refugees & Itinerant People, *Erga Migrantes Caritas Christi,* (*The love of Christ towards Migrants*), 2004.

mentality judges all religious paths as of equal validity, because truth is seen as something that only relates to the believer (that is, it is true *for that person*, and that is *all* it means). There are no objective standards of measurement, no public truth that holds good for everyone. There are many who claim that dialogue is only possible if we abandon our Christian belief that in Jesus Christ we encounter the universally valid truth about God, the God who became human, and uniquely revealed, in Christ. In the relativist view this exclusive claim about Christ rules out the very possibility of dialogue.

26. The Church rejects this relativism. The Declaration *Dominus Iesus* (*The Lord Jesus*)[12] specifically addresses this issue:

> *As a remedy for this relativistic mentality, which is becoming ever more common, it is necessary above all to reassert the definitive and complete character of the revelation of Jesus Christ. In fact, it must be firmly believed[13] that, in the mystery of Jesus Christ, the Incarnate Son of God, who is 'the way, the truth, and the life' (Jn 14:16), the full revelation of divine truth is given (DI 5).*

27. The Catholic Church's promotion of dialogue, and its respect for the freedom of all to practise their religion, does not stem from the belief that truth is relative. Quite the contrary, it stems from the conviction that truth is one and universal, that there are glimpses of that one truth and supreme good in other religions, and that it is the one God who, in his loving Providence, is the Creator of those elements of truth and goodness.

Pastoral Consequences: Our Need to Reach out to Others

28. We bishops therefore call upon Catholics to bear witness to their love of neighbour when the religious or cultural identities of minorities are the object of intolerance or prejudice. This Christian

---

[12] Congregation for the Doctrine of the Faith, *Declaration Dominus Iesus on the Unicity and Salvific Universality of Jesus Christ and the Church*, 2000.

[13] Emphasis in the original.

witness may well involve facing up to negative attitudes in ourselves as well as in others. This will not always make us popular, but we need to give a lead in reaching out to our neighbour in this way.

29. One example of this negative behaviour is an open hostility towards migrants and asylum seekers. In his encyclical *Redemptoris Missio* of 1990 Pope John Paul II drew attention to the migration of people of other religions, especially refugees, into traditionally Christian countries as an opportunity for contacts and cultural exchanges (*RM* 37). We would add that such love of neighbour is the love of the Good Samaritan, who in the parable in St Luke's Gospel (Ch.10) offered assistance to a Jew in need, despite the intense hostility between the two peoples.[14]

30. Catholics should also welcome opportunities for collaborating with members of other religions in fields where they have similar concerns and values. They should be able to engage in activities which protect human life from conception to death, in working for justice and peace and in issues concerning the good of our world as created by God. This kind of collaboration does not require a complete agreement on all matters of faith or morality.

31. Unfortunately many Catholics do not feel sufficiently confident in the knowledge of their own faith to feel they can share it. They should see this new situation as a spur to seek ways of deepening their knowledge of the Catholic faith, in order to share it, in a way appropriate to themselves, with those of other religions. At the very least a smile of greeting, a word of good wishes on religious feasts, or a gesture of sympathy in a time of sadness, can themselves carry the love of Jesus Christ, and be channels of grace without further elaboration. As the Church's teaching makes clear, dialogue is a matter of being *with* others in constructive and human ways.

---

[14] Pope Benedict XVI makes the same point, in a more general way, in his Encyclical Letter *Deus Caritas Est* (*God is Love*) 2005, 25: *The Church is God's family in the world. In this family no one ought to go without the necessities of life. Yet at the same time 'caritas-agape'* (Christ-like love) *extends beyond the frontiers of the Church. The parable of the Good Samaritan remains as a standard which imposes universal love towards the needy whom we encounter 'by chance'.* Many migrants in our country fit that description.

32. We know well that Catholics are already engaged, and generously so, in all kinds of service to their fellow men and women, in their parishes and further afield. We encourage you to extend this neighbourliness to those of other religions.

33. *Another Side:* The coming together, through widespread immigration, of people from very different backgrounds, especially when it is of such recent origin, cannot be a simple story. For example, not all immigrants or their descendants are well disposed to our society and its values, and not all asylum seekers are genuine. What is more, we have to point out in all honesty the persecution and grossly unjust behaviour against Christians and other minorities in some of the immigrants' countries of origin, and even in this country such behaviour against Christians is not unknown. Although the majority community must take the lead, holding out the hand of friendship must be a two-way process. We would justly be accused of over-simplifying a very complex issue were we to ignore these things. We do not ignore them, and we call urgently for these matters to be addressed.

34. In this country, civil authorities have the responsibility of protecting the whole population, of whatever ethnic origin, from those who have evil intent, and from those who are dedicated to the overthrow of our society and the values – many of them fundamentally Christian values - on which it is built. We all have the responsibility of supporting the authorities in these vital matters. Immigration and the seeking of asylum most certainly need to be managed with great compassion, but also with careful discernment and a lively appreciation of the social, economic and deeply human problems they can generate.

35. We cannot stress enough, however, that these realities must never be used as an excuse for blanket prejudice and hostility, which can never be right and merely make the evils worse. Christ demands that we hold out the hand of hospitality to the stranger[15]. What is more, our protests against the ill-will of others is a great deal less

---

[15] *I was a stranger and you welcomed me (Mt 25:35).*

convincing, indeed is hypocritical, if we are guilty of the same sin ourselves. All we have to do is consider our own Christian past to realise that any religion, at its most debased, can use an allegedly divine ordinance for its wicked deeds.

36. *Conclusion:* We are right, therefore, to rejoice at the great diversity of peoples within the universal Church and we respect the religious diversity of modern Britain, seeing it as an opportunity for dialogue.[16]

---

[16] The ultimate Christian hope, of course, is that all people, in their great diversity of race, culture and giftedness, will acknowledge Christ as our one God and Saviour, and will be united in him as one reconciled humanity.

Chapter 3:
DIALOGUE IN THE TEACHING OF THE CATHOLIC CHURCH

Introduction

Interreligious Dialogue: the Catholic Church's Attitude in Modern Times

37. For some years now there has been much reflection in the Catholic Church on the relationship of interreligious dialogue to its faith and teaching. In 1965, at the Second Vatican Council, the bishops issued a document, entitled *Nostra Aetate (In our Age)* which was to set the Church on a new path regarding its relations with the other religions of the world. In this they said:

> *The Church therefore urges her sons and daughters to enter with prudence and charity into discussion and collaboration with members of other religions. Let Christians, while witnessing to their own faith and way of life, acknowledge, preserve and encourage the spiritual and moral truths found among non-Christians, also their social life and culture (NA 2).*

38. One of the legacies of Pope John Paul II is the example he gave of seeking to engage with people of other religions. In his many journeys across the world he pointed out the path of dialogue. He was the first pope to enter a synagogue, and the first to enter a mosque. In 1986, 1993 and 2002 he was joined at Assisi by leaders of the world's religions, and by other Christian leaders, in order to pray for peace.

39. Pope Benedict XVI is no less committed to the way of dialogue. He is also very conscious of the deep differences between the religions, and of the need to be as clear as possible in stating the faith of the Catholic Church. In his first public address as Pope in April 2005 he said that while his first priority would be dialogue with other

Christians, his second would be interreligious dialogue.[17] When, as Cardinal Ratzinger, he was Prefect of the Congregation for the Doctrine of the Faith, it was he who was responsible for the Declaration *Dominus Iesus* in the year 2000. While it was careful to draw a clear line between Christianity and other religions, the Declaration still made this point:

> *Interreligious dialogue, which is part of the Church's evangelising mission, requires an attitude of understanding and a relationship of mutual knowledge and reciprocal enrichment, in obedience to the truth and with respect for freedom (DI 2).*

40. During his visit to Turkey in November 2006, Pope Benedict declared that dialogue was not an option but a necessity. In an address to the President of the Turkish Religious Affairs Directorate he said:

> *For more than forty years the teaching of the Second Vatican Council has inspired and guided the approach taken by the Holy See and by local churches throughout the world to relations with the followers of other religions. Following the Biblical tradition, the Council teaches that the entire human race shares a common origin and a common destiny: God, our Creator and the goal of our earthly pilgrimage. Christians and Muslims belong to the family of those who believe in the one God and who, according to their respective traditions, trace their ancestry to Abraham. The human and spiritual unity in our origins and our destiny impels us to seek a common path, as we play our part in the quest for fundamental values so characteristic of the people of our time...[18]*

---

[17] First Message of His Holiness Benedict XVI at the end of the Concelebrated Mass with the College of Cardinals, 20th April 2005. See: *http//www.vatican.va/holy_father/benedict_xvi/messages/pont-messages/2005/documents/hf_ben-xvi_mes_20050420_missa-pro-ecclesia_en.html*

[18] See: *www.vatican.va/holy_father/benedict_xvi/speeches/2006/november/documents/hf_ben-xvi_spe_20061128_pres-religious-affairs_en.html*

Resources

41. To discover the teaching of the Church on this subject we should above all refer to the documents of the Second Vatican Council, and to subsequent papal pronouncements.[19] We must also take note of certain very significant actions by the popes, because deeds can speak louder than words. Among these we mention again Pope John Paul II's invitations to multi-religious gatherings at Assisi to pray for peace, and his visits to sites held in special reverence by other religions, such as the Yad Vashem Holocaust Memorial in Jerusalem and, as a penitent, to the Western Wall in the same city. In his turn, Pope Benedict XVI has also visited the Western Wall and the Yad Vashem Memorial, and synagogues in Cologne and New York. He has paid a visit to the Blue Mosque in Istanbul, and to the Al-Hussein bin Talal Mosque in Jordan.

42. Much help can be found in the publications of the Pontifical Council for Interreligious Dialogue, such as *Dialogue and Mission* (1984), referred to above, and *Dialogue and Proclamation* (1991)[20]. The previously mentioned Declaration of the Congregation for the Doctrine of the Faith, *Dominus Iesus*, is of particular importance.

The Declaration Nostra Aetate: The special position of the Jewish People

43. The Second Vatican Council's document *Nostra Aetate*, or *Declaration on the Relation of the Church to Non-Christian Religions*, is the principal statement of the Church's teaching authority on the general subject of interreligious dialogue. It is important to note, however, that it gives a particularly developed teaching on the Church's relation to the Jews: in fact for a long time in the preparation of this statement it was simply and solely a statement about the Jews. At the time of the Council in the 1960s, the bishops remembered, in some cases all too personally, the evils of the Nazis and their unspeakable acts of genocide against the Jewish people. They were anxious to condemn unreservedly the injustices done to them, not just

---

[19] A fuller Book List is given at the end of the Document.

[20] Full title: *Reflections and Orientations on Interreligious Dialogue and the Proclamation of the Gospel of Jesus Christ* published jointly by the Pontifical Council for Interreligious Dialogue and the Congregation for Evangelisation of Peoples, Rome 1991.

in the twentieth century, but in all periods of history. They wanted to outlaw, in fact, all forms of discrimination against anyone in the name of race, colour, condition of life or religion.

44. The Council bishops wished to do more than merely condemn. They wanted to reflect positively on the unique relationship, in the mystery of God's saving love, between the Church of Christ and the Jewish people. Their teaching, the fruit of long debate, is expressed in article 4 of *Nostra Aetate*. Relying heavily on the eleventh chapter of St Paul's Epistle to the Romans, the bishops set out some guiding principles for understanding this relationship more adequately.[21]

45. They readily acknowledge that the origins of Christ's Church are deeply rooted in God's People of the Old Covenant, and in the revelation God made to them. The Church, they say *is nourished from the root of the good olive tree, on to which the branches of the wild olive tree of the gentiles have been grafted* (*Rm* 11:17). Not only Jesus himself and Mary his mother, but the apostles too, the founding pillars of the Church, and many of the first disciples were Jews. The bishops recognise that at the time of Jesus most Jews did not accept the Gospel, and many opposed it; nevertheless the Jewish people remain very dear to God, who never repents of his gifts and calling.[22] It is therefore desirable that dialogue and discussion, based on biblical and theological enquiry, should take place between the two biblical faiths.

46. Then the Council makes a statement of major doctrinal significance, i.e. as a matter of Catholic faith, and rejecting out of hand the claim so often used as an excuse for the worst persecutions, that the Jews in general, then and since, are guilty of the death of Christ, and so are an accursed people:

> *Although the Jewish authorities with their followers pressed for the death of Christ, still those things which were perpetrated during his*

---

[21] For further documents from the Holy See on Catholic-Jewish relations, see Book List.

[22] On 13th April 1986, Pope John Paul II stressed this point when, in Rome, he made the first-ever visit of a Pope to a synagogue. He called the Jews 'our dearly beloved brothers', and said, echoing Rm 11, that they were 'beloved of God' who has called them with an 'irrevocable calling', and whose covenant with them 'has never been revoked' (Gioia, p.335).

passion cannot be ascribed indiscriminately to all the Jews living at the time, nor to the Jews of today. Although the Church is the new people of God, the Jews should not be represented as rejected by God or accursed, as if that follows from holy scripture (NA 4).[23]

47. This close and unique relationship between the Church and the Synagogue was given practical expression not long after the Council. In 1974 Pope Paul VI set up the Commission for Religious Relations with the Jews, and joined it, not to the Secretariat for Non-Christians[24] but to the Secretariat for Promoting Christian Unity[25]. This gives recognition to the fact that the division between the Jewish community and the Church of Christ pre-dates the divisions within Christianity itself, and is the deepest wound within the whole People of God of the old and new Covenants. In the understanding of the Catholic Church the healing of this ancient wound is not only a matter of coming to a much greater knowledge of one another – a most urgent need in itself[26] - but of reaching out in hope towards a unity, here and now only imperfectly understood, which would be both a new gift of God and the healing of this ancient wound in his People.

48. Although it must be stated clearly that the Jewish Community and the Church of Christ are quite distinct, the relationship between them is unique. This is reflected in the fact that the Commission for Religious Relations with the Jews is housed within the Pontifical Council for Promoting Christian Unity, while remaining functionally distinct from it.[27]

---

[23] Henceforth, unless otherwise stated, translations of Vatican II documents are from Norman P. Tanner (ed.), *Decrees of the Ecumenical Councils*, Georgetown University Press, 1990, vol. II.

[24] Later the Pontifical Council for Interreligious Dialogue (see n.1 above).

[25] Later the Pontifical Council for Promoting Christian Unity.

[26] See Commission for Religious Relations with the Jews, *Guidelines on Religious Relations with the Jews*, 1974.

[27] In England and Wales there is a special committee of the Bishops' Conference for these matters, the Committee for Catholic-Jewish Relations. On the ecumenical level there is the Council of Christians and Jews, whose aim is to work against discrimination in our society.

The Broadening of the Declaration

49. The Council bishops eventually decided that their statement needed to have wider application, to encompass interreligious relations in general. The consequence was that for the first time in history a General Council of the Catholic Church recognised elements of truth and holiness in other religions as the work of the one God of salvation, and to that extent recognised the presence and work of grace in the religions of the world. In practical terms this recognition has moved the Church on to new and constructive, yet always carefully considered ways of engaging with the followers of these religions.

50. The Declaration begins thus:

> *In our age, when the human race is being daily brought closer together, and contacts between the various nations are becoming more frequent, the Church is giving closer attention to what is its relation to non-Christian religions. In its task of promoting unity and charity among people, indeed also among nations, it now turns its attention chiefly to what things human beings have in common, and what things tend to bring them together. (NA 1)*

The Church's Teaching

51. In all its teaching the Catholic Church keeps a careful balance between insisting that God truly wills the eternal salvation of all people, and insisting with equal force that Christ is the one and only means and mediator of this salvation. The Church also keeps a balance between recognising what is true and holy in other religions, and yet insisting on the importance of an explicit faith in Christ and membership of the Church through Baptism. Thus the promotion of dialogue has not diminished the necessity of proclaiming the Gospel and calling those who do not believe in Christ to conversion while fully respecting the liberty of each person.

52. In all this discussion, of course, we must never forget the fundamental truth that judgment about people's eternal salvation belongs to God, and to God alone.

53. Three themes recur constantly in the Church's teaching: the unity of the human race; the need to be open to all that is true and holy in other religions; the call to dialogue. We shall consider these in turn.

The Unity of the Human Race

54. The Church's positive attitude to people and communities belonging to other religions is based on its conviction that the human race is *one*, one through its origin in the one creative act of God, one in physical descent, one in its predicament caused by sin and need of salvation, and one in God's saving purposes. This is a profoundly biblical conviction. This is how *Nostra Aetate* puts it:

> *All nations are one community and have one origin, because God caused the whole human race to dwell on the whole face of the earth. They also have one final end, God, whose providence, manifestation of goodness and plans for salvation are extended to all... (NA 1).*

55. The unity of all humanity was very prominent in the thinking of Pope John Paul II. For him, this unity is the best place to begin when reflecting on the plurality of world religions. The unity is not merely a biological one: the Pope refers to a '*mystery* of unity', a glimpse of God's loving design for those he created in his own image and likeness. As yet we only understand a little of this divine purpose, but we do know that it is centred upon Jesus Christ, the Word made flesh, crucified and risen. In an important address to the Roman Curia after the 1986 World Day of Prayer for Peace at Assisi, he said:

> *Accordingly there is only one divine plan for every human being who comes into this world, one single origin and goal, whatever may be the colour of his skin, the historical and geographical framework within which he happens to live and act, or the culture in which he grows up and expresses himself. The differences are a less important element, when confronted with the unity which is radical, fundamental and decisive.*

The divine plan, unique and definitive, has its centre in Jesus Christ, God and man, 'in whom people find the fullness of religious life and in whom God has reconciled all things to himself' (NA 2).[28]

Human Unity and Religious Freedom

56. Since all human beings are created in God's image they all have an equal dignity as persons, as images of the personal God, with the rights and duties which flow from this. One of these rights is the right to religious freedom. The Second Vatican Council's 'Declaration on Religious Freedom', known as *Dignitatis Humanae* ('Human dignity'), makes this point very clearly:

This Vatican synod declares that the human person has a right to religious freedom. Such freedom consists in this, that all should have such immunity from coercion by individuals or by groups, or by any human power, that no one should be forced to act against his conscience in religious matters, nor prevented from acting according to his conscience, whether in private or in public, whether alone or in association with others, within due limits. This synod further declares that the right to religious freedom is firmly based on the dignity of the human person as this is known from the revealed word of God and from reason itself (DH 2).

57. The Declaration goes on to speak of our right, and our obligation, to pursue the truth in a properly human way, that is by free enquiry in accordance with our conscience. This freedom includes the right to have places of worship and religious associations.

58. All this is relevant to the whole field of interreligious relationships and dialogue. The right to religious freedom is based on our equal dignity before God; but as a basis for dialogue the recognition of this right must be *reciprocal*, because dialogue can only work properly as a dialogue between equals.

---

[28] Pope John Paul II, Address 22nd December 1986 (Gioia, p.361).

59. This equality, it must be stressed, refers to the equal dignity of the *participants*, not to equality in the *content of what they believe*. Still less does it imply a comparison between the notable men and women of the world's religions and Jesus Christ, the divine *Word made flesh* (cf. *Jn* 1:14).

Human Unity in the Questions all have in Common

60. People across the world ask the same ultimate questions about their lives, questions often asked with deep anxiety: What is the meaning and purpose of our life on earth - does it have any meaning at all? Is there a God, and if so what is God like? Why is there suffering – has it a meaning? What is the secret of true happiness? What happens after death? These common questions show how human beings are united in their restless search for meaning.

The Need to be open to what is True and Holy in other Religions

61. *Nostra Aetate* takes note of the unity people have in their questions, and gives examples of the answers the world's religions have offered, recognising elements of truth and holiness in those answers:

> *The Catholic Church rejects nothing of those things which are true and holy in these religions. It regards with respect those ways of acting and living and those precepts and teachings which, though often at variance with what it holds and expounds, frequently reflect a ray of that truth which enlightens everyone (NA 2).*

62. The Catholic Church believes that our unity is also revealed in the fact that this presence of what is true and holy is not accidental. It is what the Council calls 'a ray of the one Truth' and, in the Decree *Ad Gentes* on Missionary Activity (*To the nations*), 'seeds of the Word' (*AG* 11). In other words, the presence of what is true and holy is directly related to the revelation of Christ and to his Church. *Lumen Gentium* states:

Whatever goodness and truth is found in them is considered by the Church as a preparation for the Gospel, and bestowed by him who enlightens everyone, that they might in the end have life (LG 16).

63. The expression 'seeds of the Word' originates in the early Church Fathers, who saw the presence of true and righteous living among the pagans as a participation in the one Truth and Word who would become flesh in Christ. Foremost among these was St Justin, the Christian Apologist, martyred in about 165AD. Among many references to 'seeds of the Word' he writes: *In moral philosophy the Stoics have established right principles, and the poets too have expounded such, because the seed of the Word was implanted in the whole human race* (2 *Apol.* VIII).

Christ the only Saviour and only Source of divine Truth

64. These affirmative statements in no way lessen the Church's belief in the unique position of Christ as the incarnation and revelation of the Word of God, and the one Saviour of all. Christ is '...*the way, the truth and the life' in whom people find the fullness of religious life and in whom God has reconciled all things to himself* (*NA* 2). Christ, and he alone, is the final answer to our fundamental questions and longings.

65. Our faith in Christ gives us the assurance that whatever is true and holy in other religions is not an alternative to the Gospel, but a preparation for it. The aspirations of humanity, and the answers offered by the various religious traditions, all have their fulfilment in Jesus Christ. It is therefore essential for the Church, in faithfulness to the Gospel, to balance the affirmative statements about other religions with an honest confession of what our faith sees as lacking (that is, needing to be completed) in those religions.[29]

66. As the ancient writers put it, what is true and holy in the religions are 'a preparation for the Gospel', waiting to be healed and perfected by the word of the Gospel and the sacraments of Christ. From the viewpoint of Christian faith this 'waiting' is in some ways like the state

[29] Cf. *AG*, 9

of those living before the time of Christ, whose state of real and serious need we recall in the Church's liturgy during the season of Advent.[30]

67. This assertion that Christ is the only Saviour does not imply the superiority of individual Christians over everyone else. What Christians have received is totally unmerited on their part. It is an assertion rather of the bountiful goodness of God, and of the awesome responsibility Christians have of living up to what they have received, of being humbly thankful for it, and of being ever ready to share it with others. Jesus himself gave this warning:

> *From everyone to whom much has been given, much will be required; and from the one to whom much has been entrusted, even more will be demanded (Lk 12:48).*

The Presence of the saving Grace of Christ in other Religions

68. Christ, and Christ alone, is our Saviour: that is, he is the only way we human beings can come to our common goal in the glory and happiness of God, Father, Son and Holy Spirit. The Second Vatican Council, and subsequent papal teaching, affirm the active presence of the freely given, saving power of Christ ('grace') outside the visible, institutional confines of the Church:

> *There are those who without any fault do not know anything about Christ or his Church, yet who search for God with a sincere heart and, under the influence of grace, try to put into effect the will of God as known to them through the dictate of conscience: these too can obtain eternal salvation. Nor does divine Providence deny the helps that are necessary for salvation to those who, through no fault of their own, have not yet attained to the express recognition of God yet who strive, not without divine grace, to lead an upright life. For whatever goodness and truth is found in*

---

[30] The Declaration *Dominus Iesus* refers to this situation in *DI* 22. It expresses 'sincere respect' for the world's religions, and acknowledges that their followers can receive the grace of God, but has to say that from the standpoint of faith in Christ as the Saviour of all humanity their situation is seriously lacking ('gravely deficient') compared with the situation of those who have access to all the means of salvation in the Church. It is not the people whom *Dominus Iesus* sees as 'deficient', but their situation.

them is considered by the Church as a preparation for the Gospel,
and bestowed by him who enlightens everyone that they may in
the end have life (LG 16).

69. This grace is intimately related to Christ, the fruit of his sacrifice on the Cross, and bestowed on those outside the visible Church through the presence of the Holy Spirit. This grace of God, however, is still related to the Church. It does not make members of other religions 'Christian', but enlightens them in a way appropriate to their particular situation.

The Presence of the Holy Spirit in Members of other Religions

70. A remarkable feature of the teaching of Pope John Paul II is the prominence he gave to the activity of the Holy Spirit in the lives of those who belong to other religions. In the encyclical *Redemptoris Missio* (*Mission of the Redeemer*) he says:

The Spirit manifests himself in a special way to the Church and in her members. Nevertheless his presence and activity are universal, limited by neither space nor time.

The Spirit's presence and activity affect not only individuals but also society and history, peoples, cultures and religions. Indeed, the Spirit is at the origin of the noble ideals and undertakings which benefit humanity on its journey through history... Again, it is the Spirit who sows the 'seeds of the Word' present in various customs and cultures, preparing them for full maturity in Christ (RM 28).

71. Although the Holy Spirit's presence in history and in other religions cannot be equated with the abundance of the Spirit's gifts to the Church, it is nevertheless the same divine Spirit who is at work in them, the source of whatever is true and holy, and bringing them into a positive relationship with the Church.

72. It must be stressed that the Spirit who is active in other religions is always profoundly one with Christ, and not an alternative to Christ. He is the same Spirit who was at work in the human coming-to-be of Christ, and in Christ's life, death and resurrection. He is the Spirit bestowed on the Church at Pentecost as the fruit of Christ's passion and death (Cf. *RM* 29).

The Church-centred aspect of this Teaching

73. The Spirit, then, who is at work in other religions, and supremely in Christ himself, is one and the same Spirit who gives life to the Church. Because it is the same divine Spirit who is at work in both, the Church and the religions have a positive relationship to each other. By that God-given presence and action we are deeply related, though at the same time sadly distant from each other.

74. The Church is not only 'passively' related to other religions because of the Spirit's presence: the Church has an active role in the salvation of all people. The Church is the sign and instrument of a communion with God and with each other that begins in this life and is completed hereafter. The Church is called to work actively for this by its prayer, by its preaching, by its proclamation of the Gospel and calling people to faith in Christ, and also by interreligious dialogue.

Each Religion is related to the Church in its own Way

75. The Second Vatican Council presents the various religions as each having its own distinctive relationship to the Church.[31] It follows that our approach to each, and any dialogue with it, will have its own character. We mention here those religions present in this country in relatively larger numbers:[32]

76. Islam: Despite the fact that there are profound theological differences between the two religions, Islam shares with Christianity many common traditions and ideas, as well as a long history of both creative and hostile encounter. Although Jews, Muslims and Christians within their own respective tradition understand God and relate to him in a different way, they all worship the one God. In various different ways, all claim Abraham as their ancestor and honour his close relationship with God. For reasons that are all too obvious, it has never been more urgent that Christians and Muslims learn how to dialogue with, and better understand, one another. The Second Vatican Council speaks of Muslims in *Nostra Aetate* 3:

---

[31] Cf. *LG* 16; *NA* 3-4.

[32] The unique relationship of Judaism to the Church was explained above in nn.43 onwards.

The Church also looks upon Muslims with respect. They worship the one God living and subsistent, merciful and almighty, creator of heaven and earth, who has spoken to humanity and to whose decrees, even the hidden ones, they seek to submit themselves whole-heartedly, just as Abraham, to whom the Islamic faith readily relates itself, submitted to God. They venerate Jesus as a prophet, even though they do not acknowledge him as God, and they honour his virgin mother Mary and even sometimes devoutly call upon her. Furthermore they await the day of judgment when God will requite all people brought back to life. Hence they have regard for the moral life and worship God especially in prayer, almsgiving and fasting.

Although considerable dissensions and enmities between Christians and Muslims may have arisen in the course of the centuries, this synod urges all parties that, forgetting past things, they train themselves towards sincere mutual understanding and together maintain and promote social justice and moral values as well as peace and freedom for all people.

77. Hinduism: Hinduism is not strictly a single organised religion, but a whole family of religions rooted in the Indian sub-continent, and its members comprise over 80% of the vast and diverse population of India. There are also Hindus living in other countries around the world, including a large community in Britain. Hindus witness to our human yearning for the divine, to the importance of family life and to the possibility that different religions can live together in peace. The Second Vatican Council thus pays tribute to the ancient, profound and richly varied Hindu traditions:

…Thus in Hinduism the divine mystery is explored and propounded with an inexhaustible wealth of myths and penetrating philosophical investigations, and liberation is sought from the distresses of our state either through various forms of ascetical life or deep meditation, or taking refuge in God with loving confidence (NA 2).

78. In his first visit to India, Pope John Paul II praised the 'spiritual vision of man' at the heart of Indian religious culture:

India has so much to offer to the world in the task of understanding man and the truth of his existence. What she offers specifically is a noble spiritual vision of man – man, a pilgrim of the Absolute, travelling toward a goal, seeking the face of God. Did not Mahatma Gandhi put it this way: 'What I want to achieve – what I have been striving and pining to achieve…is self-realisation – to see God face to face. I live and move and have my being in pursuit of this goal.'[33]

Despite all the powerful forces of poverty and oppression, of evil and sin in all their forms, the power of truth will prevail – the truth about God, the truth about man. It will prevail because it is invincible. The power of truth is invincible! 'Satyam eva jayate – truth alone triumphs', as the motto of India proclaims.[34]

79. Buddhism: For Christians, dialogue with Buddhists is quite different from dialogue with Jews or Muslims because no personal creator God plays a significant part in Buddhism. What makes Buddhists what they are is not a creed, nor even primarily the ascetical practices they follow, but rather their personal commitment to search for truth as the Buddha[35] did. Buddhism has attracted many in the West because of its high moral standards, its teaching about meditation, its commitment to compassion, peace and justice, and its great respect for nature and the environment. *Nostra Aetate* affirms:

In Buddhism, according to its various forms, the radical inadequacy of this changeable world is acknowledged and a way is taught whereby those with a devout and trustful spirit may be able to reach either a state of perfect freedom or, relying on their own efforts or on help from a higher source, the highest illumination (NA 2).

---

[33] Address to the Followers of the Various Religions of India, 1986. Cf. Gioia p.314, with the reference to Mahatma Gandhi, *Autobiography*, pp 4-5.

[34] Gioia p.315, with reference to *Mundaka Upanishad*, 3,1,6.

[35] The Buddha ('enlightened one'), is the title given to Siddartha Gautama, who scholars now reckon to have been born in N.India in about 480 B.C.

80. Pope John Paul II reinforced this on a visit to Korea in 1984:

...the Korean people throughout history have sought, in the great ethical and religious visions of Buddhism and Confucianism, the path to the renewal of self and to the consolidation of the whole people in virtue and in nobility of purpose. The profound reverence for life and nature, the quest for truth and harmony, self-abnegation and compassion, the ceaseless striving to transcend – these are among the noble hallmarks of your spiritual tradition that have led, and will continue to lead, the nation and the people through turbulent times to the haven of peace.

Our diversity in religious and ethical beliefs calls upon all of us to foster genuine fraternal dialogue and to give special consideration to what human beings have in common and to what promotes fellowship among them...[36]

81. Sikhism: Sikhism originates from the Punjab in Northern India, and there is now a considerable Sikh community in this country which is one of the largest outside India itself. The Sikhs are open to interreligious dialogue, very much in the spirit of their founder Guru Nanak (b.1469 AD). Excellent relations have been formed between Sikhs and Christians, including Catholics, in various parts of the country. Their religion differs from Christianity in many respects, but they believe in one God the Creator, and in the equality of all human beings as God's creatures irrespective of earthly rank or position, and they have a strong tradition of service and hospitality.

82. Other Religions: We have mentioned the religions whose members are present in this country in relatively large numbers, and of course are to be found in much larger numbers elsewhere. In Britain today, however, there are many more religions than this: there are the Zoroastrians, the Jains and the Baha'is, who originate in India or the Near East, and some of the traditional religions of Africa are also represented.

---

[36] Address to the Leaders of the Various Religions of Korea, 1984. Cf. Gioia p.278.

83. These religions in their great variety have developed their own patterns of thought and practice, and they will each stand in a different relationship to the Church. A particular dialogue, perhaps a local one, between some of them and the Catholic Church could well be appropriate and fruitful. The diocesan bishop, and the Bishops' Conference, should be consulted on what dialogues are being encouraged by the Church, and what form they should take.

The Church's Call to Dialogue

84. The call to dialogue is a practical consequence of the Church's belief in the unity of the human race, and in the God-given presence of truth and holiness in other religions. Through dialogue we 'meet God in Friend and Stranger', and through dialogue the Stranger can become a Friend. But this call *by* the Church is also a response to the God who calls *to* the Church. We must be sensitive to the signs of the times: God calls to the Church through the passing events of history, and in particular through the features so characteristic of our own time, the greater closeness of peoples thanks to modern communication and, as far as Europe is concerned, the migration of people of other religions into the traditionally Christian West.

85. Dialogue, therefore, has become part of the contemporary Catholic Church's understanding of her Christ-given mission to be the sign and instrument of uniting all people to God and to each other. It is not optional, and is intrinsic to our understanding of the Church today.

Dialogue and the Evangelising Mission of the Church

Interreligious dialogue is part of the Church's evangelising mission. Understood as a means of mutual knowledge and enrichment dialogue is not in opposition to the mission 'ad gentes'; indeed it has special links with that mission and is one of its expressions.[37]

---

[37] *RM* 55.

86. These words of Pope John Paul II in *Redemptoris Missio* may well puzzle many Christians, Catholics included. How can dialogue with another religion and its set of beliefs possibly be part of evangelisation? The reason is that 'evangelisation' does not only mean explicitly proclaiming Jesus Christ and calling followers of other religions or unbelievers to conversion. That indeed is the climax of the evangelising mission, obeying Christ's missionary mandate *Go into all the world and proclaim the good news to all creation* (*Mk* 16:15); but the work of evangelisation is much wider than that. Christians evangelise, and the Church as such evangelises, whenever by Christ's power and the Holy Spirit, in any way whatever, they enable the Reign or Kingdom of God to permeate the minds and hearts, the cultures and activities of the world of their time. Jesus himself, after all, did not only proclaim the 'Good News of the Kingdom of God' by his powerful words and his mighty acts, but also by his very presence and behaviour, by everything he said and did. When by his grace Christians live according to the Gospel and its values, they are evangelising, and so bringing Christ's saving presence into their world.[38]

87. The principal form of evangelisation, and what all evangelising activity points towards, is what the Catholic Church nowadays calls *Proclamation:* proclaiming Christ crucified and risen as God and Saviour, calling those who do not believe in Christ to faith in him and to conversion of life, and inviting them to enter the community of the Church by Baptism, Confirmation and the Holy Eucharist. This activity is often called 'evangelism' by our fellow Christians. However, among all the other forms of evangelisation there is also that of doing what *Nostra Aetate* recommended:

> *Let Christians, while witnessing to their own faith and way of life, acknowledge, preserve and encourage the spiritual and moral truths found among non-Christians, also their social life and culture (NA 2).*

---

[38] Pope Paul VI made this clear in his Apostolic Exhortation *Evangelii Nuntiandi* (*Proclaiming the Gospel*) 1975, 17-20, where he warns against too narrow a view of evangelisation.

88. Dialogue is an example of what *Nostra Aetate* is recommending, and it clearly helps to unite people more closely in communion with God and with each other. Dialogue is an aspect of the Church's whole mission to be the 'sacrament' of this communion, and a vital part of evangelisation.

89. We cannot emphasise too strongly that *interreligious dialogue is not a covert form of proselytism* (dishonest or aggressive persuasion). It is, as we have said, part of evangelisation, which is a wide group of activities whose primary example is admittedly proclamation, but it is still distinct from proclamation. In dialogue we are not trying by underhand means to convert the other person. Dialogue is an honest witnessing to our belief, and a sincere listening to the belief of the other person. A Christian who loves Our Lord, and truly believes in him, and whose friendship with the dialogue partner is genuine, will of course desire and pray that through dialogue Christ will be better known, recognised and indeed loved; how could he/she not desire it and, as part of the honest witnessing, say frankly to the other that this is his/her prayer? Partners in dialogue may well say the same, in terms of their own religion, to the Christian.[39] That does not make the dialogue dishonest; in fact it ensures its sincerity.

90. Indeed, the entire love-story of God's relationship to humanity can be thought of as a dialogue: Pope Paul VI called it the *dialogue of salvation*.[40] It can be imagined as a conversation initiated by the Father and conducted with human beings through Christ by the Holy Spirit active in the world. The Church's mission is to carry on that dialogue and make it accessible to all. Interreligious dialogue is a continuation, knowingly or unknowingly by those involved, of that divine dialogue.

91. Such striving for dialogue is part of the Church's mission, even if at times it is not welcome, nor met with a corresponding attitude in others. The Church is simply being faithful to the task the Lord has laid upon it.

---

[39] Cf. Pope John Paul II: *Interreligious dialogue cannot simply replace proclamation, but remains oriented towards proclamation. This missionary duty, moreover, does not prevent us from approaching dialogue **with an attitude of profound willingness to listen**. Apostolic Letter Novo Millennio Ineunte (At the beginning of the New Millennium)* 2001, 56. The emphasis is the Pope's own.

[40] *Ecclesiam Suam*, 70-77.

92. We could put this in another way. Dialogue with our brothers and sisters of other religions is obeying the command to love our neighbour. The parable of the Good Samaritan (*Lk* 10:25-37) reminds us that this means being a neighbour to the religious 'other', and by so doing manifesting and putting into effect God's saving love for all his children.

The Spirit and Motivation of Dialogue

93. One obvious and pragmatic motive for dialogue is the danger the world faces from violence and terrorism. Religious divisions play a significant part in these tensions today, and debased forms of religion are sometimes used by the perpetrators as an excuse for their crimes. Religion's detractors regularly lay the blame for these crimes at religion's door. In January 2001, the year that was to see the September 11th attack on the United States, Pope John Paul II wrote these prophetic words:

> *...the Church has sought to build ...a relationship of openness and dialogue with the followers of other religions. This dialogue must continue...it is obvious that this dialogue will be specially important in establishing a sure basis for peace, and warding off the dread spectre of those wars of religion which have so often bloodied human history.*[41]

94. Pope Benedict XVI, no less than his predecessor, sees the pursuit of world peace as a pressing motive for dialogue. On the occasion of World Youth Day at Cologne in 2005, he spoke to an invited group of Muslims:

> *Interreligious and intercultural dialogue between Christians and Muslims cannot be reduced to an optional extra. It is in fact a vital necessity, on which in large measure our future depends.*[42]

---

[41] *Novo Millennio Ineunte*, 55.

[42] Apostolic Journey to Cologne, on the Occasion of the 20th World Youth Day, Meeting with Representatives of some Muslim Communities, *Address of His Holiness Pope Benedict XVI*, Saturday, 20th August 2005.

Since then the Pope has spoken frequently and strongly on the link between interreligious dialogue and the peace of the world.

95. The longing for peace is of course shared by all people of good will, Christian or not. For a Christian, however, the love of one's neighbour and the desire for the unity of humanity in Christ is a further motive, based on our Christian faith. Our faith, in fact, takes us even further, into the radical Christian spirituality of 'putting on Christ', carrying his Cross, and following him through death to resurrection. St Paul puts this very clearly:

> *I want to know Christ and the power of his resurrection, and the sharing of his sufferings by becoming like him in his death, if somehow I may attain the resurrection from the dead (Ph 3:10-11).*

96. The Christian approach to dialogue is at its heart an entering into the costly love of Christ for humanity, which reached its fullest expression in the story of his Passion from Gethsemane to the Cross. This story is not only a human story, though it is most certainly that; it is the story of God's own involvement in our story, a God we confess to be Father, Son and Spirit.

97. It was God the Son, made flesh in Jesus,

> *…who, though he was in the form of God, did not regard equality with God a thing to be exploited, but emptied himself…and being found in human form he humbled himself and became obedient to the point of death, even death on a cross (Ph 2:6-8).*

98. It was the Son, in his human nature, who *loved us, and gave himself for us (Ga* 2:20). It was the Father who *was in Christ, reconciling the world to himself* (2 Co 5:19). It is the Holy Spirit, bestowed upon the Church at Pentecost, who gives the Christian the inner motivation and power to follow Christ and to strive for dialogue with followers of other religions. It is the Holy Spirit who is the hidden source of all that is true and holy in them, and so provides the common ground where each can reach out to the other.

> *In this dialogue of salvation, Christians and others are called to collaborate with the Spirit of the risen Lord who is universally*

present and active. Interreligious dialogue does not merely aim at mutual understanding and friendly relations. It reaches a much deeper level, that of the spirit, where exchange and sharing consist in a mutual witness to one's beliefs and a common exploration of one's respective religious convictions.[43]

99. Dialogue follows naturally from the Catholic Church's Christ-centred and Church-centred view of other religions. By discovering what is true and holy in them, we discover the relationship each has to Christ and the Church. In dialogue we must not be surprised, but actually expect to find that God is already there, and that Christ has gone before us with 'seeds of the Word'. It is in dialogue that we meet and are moved to collaborate with the same Holy Spirit we have received ourselves.

100. We have referred in the previous paragraphs to God the Holy Trinity, and spoken of Christ as the Son of God. These words draw attention to that which is most characteristic and fundamental about our Christian faith: we believe in the one God as Trinity, Father, Son and Spirit, and in Jesus Christ as the Son who became a human being, was crucified and is now risen. This belief makes us what we are. Interreligious dialogue must never try to smooth out or put to one side the irreducible differences that exist between the religions. They cannot be reduced to one and the same, although it is certainly one and the same God who is at work in the elements of truth and holiness within them.

The Spirit and Motivation of Dialogue with 'the other' as 'other'

101. Of course, part of the function of dialogue is to clear away misunderstandings and establish in a precise manner points of convergence and of divergence, so that we can then encounter one another's religion as it truly is. But that is only the beginning – it is only the overture to dialogue. Real dialogue begins when we encounter the irreducible 'otherness' of the other religion, and are led to identify not only what, from our Christian perspective, we must reject as false in it,

---

[43] Pontifical Council for Interreligious Dialogue, *Dialogue & Proclamation*, 1991, 40.

but also to grasp at the fringes of God's unsearchable mystery, his transcendent Otherness, in the presence of elements of truth and holiness in the very strangeness of what our dialogue-partner believes and stands for. God, who is *the* Other, will always be greater than our thought of him. Dialogue should make us exclaim with St Paul, when he was confronted with the mystery of God's ways:

> *O the depth of the riches and wisdom and knowledge of God! How unsearchable are his judgments and how inscrutable his ways! 'For who has known the mind of the Lord? Or who has been his counsellor?' 'Or who has given a gift to him, to receive a gift in return?' For from him and through him and to him are all things. To him be glory for ever. Amen (Rm 11:33-36).*

102. Although, as Pope John Paul II said, *the Kingdom cannot be detached either from Christ or from the Church (RM* 18), God does not restrict himself to his visible Church, which is the 'sacrament', the privileged sign and instrument of the Kingdom but not simply identical with it. So Church and Kingdom are distinct, yet they are not separate. The Church, sacrament of the Kingdom, has the mission of announcing and inaugurating the Kingdom among all peoples.[44] So dialogue should not only lead to a deeper knowledge of God and his Kingdom, but also to a deeper understanding of the Church, its sign and instrument.

The Spirit and Motivation of Dialogue: Prudence and Charity

> *The Church urges all her sons and daughters to enter with prudence and charity into discussion and collaboration with members of other religions (NA 2).*

103. Nostra Aetate here calls us to enter dialogue 'with prudence'. For dialogue to make real progress there must be no attempt at compromise, at watering down what we believe, in order to make the conversation run more smoothly:

> *Those engaged in this dialogue must be consistent with their own religious traditions and convictions, and be open to*

---

[44] Cf. *LG* 5.

understanding those of the other party without pretence or closed-mindedness, knowing that dialogue can enrich each side. There must be no abandonment of principles or false irenicism, but instead a witness given and received for mutual advancement on the road of religious enquiry and experience, and at the same time for the elimination of prejudice, intolerance and misunderstandings. Dialogue leads to inner purification and conversion which, if pursued with docility to the Holy Spirit, will be spiritually fruitful (RM 56).

104. It should be obvious from all we have said that in any deeper and more continuous kind of spiritual dialogue[45] both sides need to be thoroughly well grounded and formed in their own religious tradition. They have to have outgrown defensiveness and the desire to please, both of which spring from insecurity and plain ignorance. It is when they are well-versed and mature in their respective religious traditions that they can open themselves to the God who can always surprise us. The Spirit, like the wind, can 'blow where he wills'[46] and, as Pope John Paul put it, *is mysteriously present in every human heart (RM 29).*

105. *Nostra Aetate* speaks of prudence, but it also adds 'with charity'. Charity is the greatest of all the virtues (1 *Co* 13:13). It is only when honest witnessing is combined with a humble and respectful listening that God can come to us anew, and the Kingdom of God grow within us like a mustard seed; so true listening requires both charity and humility. It also demands self-discipline: Pope John Paul II spoke above of 'inner purification and conversion'. This can only happen if, by the grace of the Spirit, we open ourselves to the God who is beyond our thought, and who can come to us in such surprising ways. Indeed, for a Christian, the impulse to be open to others and place ourselves at their service is inspired by the example of Christ's own reconciling love. St Paul writes:

For the love of Christ urges us on, because we are convinced that one has died for all, so that those who live might live no

---

[45] See above, n.4.

[46] Cf. *Jn* 3:8.

longer for themselves, but for him who died and was raised for them (2 Co 5:14-15).

Spirit and Motivation of Dialogue: Dialogue as an expression of Hope

106. For a Christian to enter dialogue with someone of another religion is not only an expression of the Christian virtue of charity or love of neighbour: it is also a lively expression of *hope*. By this we mean hope and trust in the God whose will it is to bring all human beings to salvation, and who, in Christ and the Holy Spirit, is already at work in all that is true and holy in other religions. In these present days this loving God is calling the Church to take the path of dialogue, as part of its mission to work for the greater communion of human beings with one another and with God. This communion, the Kingdom or Reign of God, has its beginnings here and now, and will reach its completion, we believe, in a fullness of life and communion beyond this earthly life. That, in summary form, is our Christian hope, and it is precisely that hope which motivates the work of dialogue.[47]

Cooperating with our Ecumenical Partners

107. Joint work with our fellow Christians in the field of dialogue with other religions is a most valuable form of ecumenical and spiritual cooperation. By so doing we 'face outwards' together, from our common Christian faith, to the other great religions of the world, and deepen our level of communion in Christ. An example of this would be working together, in collaboration with other religions, over matters of justice, peace and the environment, or over respect for minority communities. The Pontifical Council for Promoting Christian Unity, in its 1993 Ecumenical Directory, stresses the importance of such ecumenical cooperation.[48]

---

[47] See Pope Benedict XVI's reflection on hope in his 2007 Encyclical Letter *Spe Salvi* (*In hope we were saved*).

[48] *Directory for the Application of Principles and Norms on Ecumenism*, 210. The national Council of Christians and Jews, for example, has on the Christian side the Archbishop of Canterbury, the Archbishop of Westminster and other Christian leaders as Presidents; the Christian-Muslim Forum has an ecumenical presidency on the Christian side; see also Churches Together in Britain & Ireland, Churches Together in England and Cytûn (Churches Together in Wales).

Forms of Dialogue: Discussion and Collaboration

108. *Nostra Aetate* urges us to enter into *discussion and collaboration* with members of other religions. Both discussion and collaboration are expressions of the Church's mission. By discussion we discover and respond to the presence of the true and the holy; by collaboration we work together for the greater recognition of the dignity and unity of all human beings.

109. In recent years the Church has been accustomed to refer to this discussion and collaboration by distinguishing four interdependent forms of dialogue:

The Dialogue of Life

110. This is when people of different religions simply try to live in an open and neighbourly way with one another, in the same town or street, or in the same place of work. Obviously this is not restricted to religious believers, nor need it be anything sophisticated, but when believers practise this out of their own faith-conviction it is a most effective form of dialogue. After all, 'the Church urges *all* her sons and daughters' to 'enter into discussion and collaboration'. To do this what matters is not so much the level of one's religious formation as the quality of one's faith.

The Dialogue of Action

111. This is where those of different religions collaborate in working for greater human freedom and development, such as in matters of peace, justice and the integrity of creation.

The Dialogue of Theological Exchange

112. Here specialists and scholars seek to deepen their understanding of one another's religious heritage, and their appreciation of one another's spiritual values.

The Dialogue of Religious Experience

113. In this dialogue believers who are well grounded and formed in their own religious tradition share their spiritual riches, e.g. regarding prayer and contemplation, faith, and ways of searching for God or the Absolute.[49]

114. Whatever the form of dialogue, it is important that Christians enter it aware of their Christian identity and humbly confident in it, so that dialogue will enrich their understanding and living of their faith. At the same time, dialogue is not just about academic, theological or spiritual matters. It is also, and most importantly, about living together and collaborating in the promotion of human dignity and welfare. We quoted Pope John Paul II earlier when he spoke about dialogue as *...not so much an idea to be studied as a way of living in a positive relationship with others.*[50]

Conclusion: How new is this Teaching?

115. There can be no doubt that the present-day Catholic Church's promotion of interreligious dialogue has marked a new departure, setting the Church on a new path. Yet, even though this more positive attitude is new, it still has roots in Scripture. God speaks through events, and throughout the Church's history the development of its understanding of revelation has been prompted by the new challenges and crises that the successive centuries have brought with them. Such is our present age, with its revolution in communication and in the shrinking of our world. We can see how God is thus inviting the Church to re-consider her relationship to those religions hitherto regarded in a negative or very distant way, and by dialogue with them to enter more deeply into the riches of *the faith once for all delivered to the saints (Jude 3).*

---

[49] Cf. *Dialogue and Proclamation* 42.

[50] See above, n. 2.

116. We have explained that the pursuit of dialogue stems from our belief that humanity is one, and that elements of truth and holiness are present in other religions. Both these convictions are found in Scripture, though they are nothing like as prominent, or as frequently voiced, as the contrasting conviction that both the people of the Old Covenant and the Church of Christ are the privileged beneficiaries of the unmerited choice and self-revelation of the one and only true God. For the Church this self-revelation culminated in Jesus Christ, the Son of God who became a human being.

117. This conviction has been so overwhelming, and so necessary to uphold against the surrounding idolatrous cultures from which Israel and the Church had to distance themselves at all costs, that quieter and less frequent voices of Scripture can easily be overlooked. Warnings such as that of *Ps* 113/115, *Their idols are silver and gold, the work of human hands... their makers will come to be like them, and so will all who trust in them*, and the oracles in the Prophets against the nothingness of the gods of the 'nations', are far more common than the more affirmative statements.

118. In point of fact, the insight that humanity is one, in its origins, in its sharing the one earth with a common responsibility for it, in its predicament caused by sin, and in its still being loved by the same saving God, goes right back to the earliest part of the Bible, in the creation stories themselves, and in the covenants with Noah before and after the Flood. In the Noah story, told in *Genesis* 6-9, all humanity is wiped out except for the righteous Noah and his family. With these survivors (i.e. the whole human race) God makes a covenant and promise of life: *never again shall all flesh be cut off by the waters of a flood* (9:11). God's life-giving love is for all.

119. From Chapter 12 of *Genesis*, the call of Abraham begins to separate out the people of Israel. But even here the universal application of God's salvation is clear when God promises to Abraham, *by your offspring shall all the nations of the earth gain blessing for themselves, because you have obeyed my voice* (22:18). The 'nations' are not forgotten, but are still the object of the loving designs of God, designs that are to be carried out through Abraham's offspring.

120. There was a recognition that God's grace was at work among the Gentiles in such stories as that of Melchisedech in *Gn* 14. Melchisedech is not of Abraham's people, so not an object of the special covenant that God was making with them; yet he is called *a priest of God most High*, and Abraham pays him due honour and receives a blessing. Then there is the story of the heroic Job, no Israelite yet portrayed as a model of trust in God despite the dark mystery of his innocent suffering. There is the story of the pagan city of Nineveh in the Book of Jonah (Ch.3) which repented at his preaching. Among the Prophets, Malachi condemns the Israelite priests for their slovenly irreverence, comparing them unfavourably to the nations: *From the rising of the sun to its setting my name is great among the nations* (*Ml* 1:11). Such examples suggest that although it was not at the front of their minds, Israel did realise, however intermittently, that God's love was at work elsewhere.

121. Jesus himself declares with reference to the earthly phase of his mission that he was *sent only to the lost sheep of the tribe of Israel* (*Mt* 10:6); but his salvific mission is universal and he sent his apostles to preach the Gospel to every person (cf. *Mt* 28:19-20). He warmly praises the faith of the centurion (*Mt* 8:10) and of the Syrophoenician woman (*Mt* 15:28). The Gospels clearly take it for granted that saving faith was already at work outside the Chosen People.

122. The full truth of this comes home in the earliest days of the Church. In *The Acts of the Apostles*, after the centurion Cornelius receives the Holy Spirit, St Peter exclaims:

> *I truly understand that God shows no partiality, but in every nation anyone who fears him and does what is right is acceptable to him (10:34).*

123. St Paul's speech to the Athenians in *Acts* 17, largely unsuccessful though it was, implies that in his view the religions of the nations are not entirely without value, and in Jesus Christ reach their fulfilment:

> *Athenians, I see how extremely religious you are in every way. For as I went through the city and looked carefully at the objects of your worship I found among them an altar with the inscription,*

'To an unknown god'. What therefore you worship as unknown, this I proclaim to you (17:23).

124. Later in the same speech, having declared that God made all nations *from one ancestor* he says how God:

Allotted the times of their existence and the boundaries of the places where they would live, so that they would search for God and perhaps grope for him and find him...though indeed he is not far from each one of us (17:26-27).

125. St John, in the opening chapter of his Gospel, summarises the whole Biblical teaching on the ongoing work of grace among the nations:

What has come into being in him [the Word] was life, and the life was the light of all people. The light shines in the darkness, and the darkness did not overcome it (1:3-5).

126. In the Church's history there has been the same priority given to the old and new People of God as the recipients of a uniquely personal revelation of God and his will, together with a rejection of polytheism, idolatry and many other beliefs and practices of other religions. The Church today still rejects these things. Even so, over the centuries recognition was occasionally given to God's saving activity outside the Church. We have mentioned the early Fathers' references to 'seeds of the Word' and 'rays of the one Truth' which they found in their pagan culture, and which they saw as 'preparations for the Gospel'. Much later, when the Jesuit missionaries Matteo Ricci and Roberto de Nobili travelled to the East in the sixteenth and seventeenth centuries, they were impressed by some of the aspects of the ancient cultures and religions they encountered in China and India, seeing in them elements of truth and holiness.

127. These affirmations do not amount to an endorsement of what we know as interreligious dialogue: that would be an anachronism. But it does show that the truths on which today's Catholic Church builds its teaching are quietly present in its Scriptures, in its Tradition and in its history.

A Note on 'Neo-Paganism' and 'New Age' Spirituality

128. The major traditional religions, including Christianity, originated far from these shores, but alongside these is another set of religious practices, the various branches of pagan religion. In some areas pagan traditions have never really faded away, but a major factor in the revival of paganism has been a reaction against Judaism and, even more, against Christianity. This reaction is often, but not essentially, linked to the growth of ecology and 'green' politics. The pagan calendar and rites are closely bound up with nature, and in some cases involve not only a love and respect for nature, but worship of natural forces in the shape of Mother Earth or Gaia. It poses an interesting challenge to us Christians as we grow increasingly aware of our responsibility to care for the environment, though in our case our concern for creation stems from our belief that everything around us is the beautiful handiwork of God: "God saw everything that he had made, and indeed, it was very good" (*Gn* 1:31).

129. Some more recent spiritual trends are linked to pagan religion, but are known more correctly as 'Neo-Paganism'. These have been founded relatively recently, and tend to reject the Judaeo-Christian heritage quite explicitly. The largest of these movements is Wicca, which dates from the 1950s, but what affects Christians in the British Isles most in the current revival of indigenous religious traditions is so-called 'Celtic' spirituality, which is not always as close to Christianity as people presume it to be.

130. *'New Age' Spirituality*[51]: In the last few decades, the 'New Age' movement has changed the spiritual landscape markedly. Many people have moved away from organised 'mainstream' religion to 'spirituality', a much vaguer and more fluid concept that allows

---

[51] Among many Christian reflections on the 'New Age' see *Jesus Christ, the Bearer of the Water of Life*, produced jointly by the Pontifical Council for Culture and the Pontifical Council for Interreligious Dialogue. Catholic Truth Society, 2003. See also *Proceedings of the International Consultative Meeting on New Age* (*Pro Manuscripto*, Vatican, 2008, organised in 2004 by the Congregation for the Evangelization of Peoples, the Pontifical Council for Promoting Christian Unity, the Pontifical Council for Interreligious Dialogue, and the Pontifical Council for Culture.)

them to pick and choose what they like from different religions. The New Age Movement is a complex phenomenon which is constantly changing and very hard to define. It is symptomatic of the relativistic view spoken of earlier, that all religions are of equal value and that no one religion, not even Christianity, can legitimately claim to be of unique worth.

131. A common theme running through 'New Age' spirituality is the desire for a radically new world. Sometimes this vision of a new future is expressed in the astrological claim that we live in the Age of Pisces, which has been dominated by Christianity, but a momentous change is about to take place early in the third Millennium, when the 'Age of Pisces' will be replaced by the New Age, the 'Age of Aquarius'.

132. 'New Age' cannot be called a religion – indeed it claims to supersede religion – but it is often a response to people's religious needs. Its appeal is to people who are trying to discover a spiritual dimension in their lives, and who feel that organised religion does not provide it.

133. Both Neo-Paganism and New Age are a challenge to the Church to listen to the often unspoken cry in people's hearts, and to present Jesus Christ as the one who hears that cry and can answer it. The 'Dialogue' with both of these is really a dialogue with the deepest spiritual needs of our contemporary world, and is a fundamental part of evangelisation. The Church is called to meet these expressions of that fundamental search. The practice of discernment is essential in every new expression of the religious quest. The Church's criteria for discerning what is of God, is that it leads to faith in Jesus.

Chapter 4:
PRAYER AND WORSHIP

At Assisi, in an extraordinary way, there was the discovery of the unique value that prayer has for peace. It was seen that it is impossible to have peace without prayer, the prayer of all, each one in his own identity and in search of the truth. In deepening what we have said, one must see in this another wonderful manifestation of that unity which binds us together, beyond the differences and divisions which are known to all. Every authentic prayer is under the influence of the Spirit "who intercedes insistently for us...because we do not even know how to pray as we ought", but he prays in us "with unutterable groanings" and "the one who searches hearts knows what are the desires of the Spirit" (*Rm* 8:26-27). We can indeed maintain that every authentic prayer is called forth by the Holy Spirit, who is mysteriously present in the heart of every person.

This too was seen at Assisi: the unity that comes from the fact that every man and woman is capable of praying, that is of submitting oneself totally to God and of recognising oneself to be poor in front of him. Prayer is one of the means to realise the plan of God among men.

In this way it was seen that the world cannot give peace, but that peace is a gift of God, and that it is necessary to entreat it of him by means of the prayers of all.[52]

The Desire for Multi-religious Prayer

134. When people of different religions meet together in dialogue, there is sometimes a wish to pray. This is often called 'Multi-religious Prayer'. In addition, celebrations such as marriages or funerals are times when we can find ourselves present at the prayer and worship

---

[52] Pope John Paul II, Address, 22nd December 1986, (Gioia, pp.365-6).

of other religions. Natural disasters or human conflict can also be a powerful incentive for coming together in prayer. When friendship develops between individuals or groups of different religious traditions it is natural to invite one another to our places and services of worship.

The Model of Pope John Paul II at Assisi

135. In his address to the Roman Curia quoted above, Pope John Paul II explains that his initiative of inviting all religions to Assisi in order to pray for peace was rooted in his conviction that *every authentic prayer is called forth by the Holy Spirit, who is mysteriously present in the heart of every person.*

136. This perception that every authentic prayer is the Holy Spirit's activity means that all genuine prayer is in fact the work of Father, Son and Holy Spirit, the one God at work within us. It is the Father, through the risen Christ, who bestows the Spirit when we are moved to pray; and when we pray it is in fact the Spirit prompting us to pray to the Father through the one Mediator, the risen Lord Jesus Christ. It follows then that although other religions are not Christian, and we must not call them such, they are in the Spirit related to the Church in one and the same movement of prayer, prompted by the Spirit, through Christ to the Father. When, as at Assisi, the Catholic Church comes together with other churches, ecclesial communities and other religions to pray for peace it is eloquently carrying out its mission to be the 'sacrament' of uniting all people to God and to each other, in prayer. The initiative of Pope John Paul II was indeed prophetic and instructive.

137. There is an old Latin saying, *lex orandi, lex credendi* (our prayer is an expression and ratification of our belief). For that reason we cannot literally pray together, because prayer is an expression of faith, and we do not share one faith. Nevertheless, interreligious dialogue is not just between people who believe, but between people who *pray*. This fact binds us together, even though we may be radically different in our belief, and we must respect each other's prayer just as we must respect each other's belief. In spite of our differences the way ahead must be one of prayer. We must pray *for* one another and, in the one Spirit beyond the reach of our understanding, pray in solidarity *with* one another.

'We don't come to pray together - we come together to pray'

138. The meetings at Assisi remain a model and an inspiring example of what we can do. The guiding principle at Assisi, and a guide for us, is 'We don't come to pray together, but we come together to pray'. As each religion prays, thus expressing its own faith, the others do not join in: they respect and silently give encouragement to those who are praying, and are in quiet solidarity with them on the basis of their own belief, and of the inner prayer that flows from it.

139. Catholics should thus feel confident, and be encouraged to 'come together to pray' with those of other religions. To take part in such occasions is an authentically Christian act, serving to promote the unity of all people, and their unity with God. It is part of the mission of the Church. Such prayer is an expression of love for our neighbour, and of respect for the integrity of the religions involved, and shows attentiveness to the universal presence of the Holy Spirit.

The Christian Perception of Prayer and Multi-Religious Prayer

Prayer

140. The Christian understanding of prayer is essentially Trinitarian, as we have made clear. What is more, we see prayer as never separate from the inner life of the Church, a life which is no less than the active presence of the indwelling Spirit of God. It is the Spirit who since Pentecost has united Christian believers to their risen Lord Jesus Christ, the Mediator with the Father:

> *When the work which the Father gave the Son to do on earth was accomplished, the Holy Spirit was sent on the day of Pentecost in*

order that he might continually sanctify the Church, and that consequently those who believe might have access, through Christ, in one Spirit, to the Father.[53]

141. Whether we are conscious of this or not, the 'movement' of prayer is that we pray to the Father, through the Son, in the Holy Spirit. At its deepest level, prayer is the action of the Holy Spirit within us, enabling us to respond to God's loving dialogue with us. It is God, the Holy Spirit, who always, so to speak, 'makes the first move'. He is, as the poet Francis Thompson put it, 'The Hound of Heaven'. The Catholic Catechism says:

Man may forget his Creator or hide from his face; he may run after idols or accuse the deity of having abandoned him; yet the living and true God tirelessly calls each person to that mysterious encounter known as prayer. In prayer, the faithful God's initiative of love always comes first: our own first step is always a response.[54]

142. This work of God in us takes place first and foremost in the public liturgy of the Church, but it is also at the heart of private prayer. In both of these, Christians proclaim and make more real their identity as the 'Body of Christ', branches of the one 'Vine'.[55]

Multi-religious Prayer

143. In multi-religious prayer, believers from different religions use prayers from their own tradition in the presence of the other religious groups. It should be noted that multi-religious prayer is a delicate issue, doctrinally and pastorally, and should be approached with thought and care.

144. There are two main forms of this prayer. The first is when one religion plays host to the other(s) in its own place of worship, and the second is when the religions come together in response to events, such as to the tragic event of 11th September 2001, or at a Holocaust Memorial service, or in celebration of some civic occasion.

---

[53] *LG* 4.

[54] *Catechism of the Catholic Church*, 1994, no.2567

[55] Cf. *Col* 1:18, etc; *Jn* 15:4-5.

145. *Accepting Hospitality:* To visit one another's places of worship is a way of offering or accepting hospitality, but it is also a way of advancing in understanding. Catholic schools and parish communities might profitably visit such places in their neighbourhood, and in turn welcome others to their churches and institutions. As well as fostering mutual understanding and respect, such visits can be quite profound experiences in themselves. An outstanding example of this was in November 2006, when Pope Benedict XVI visited the Blue Mosque in Istanbul and in a respectful posture, observed a moment of silence. As things turned out this symbolic act of prayer became the crowning moment of his visit to Turkey, and was a source of healing and blessing for Catholic-Muslim relations.

146. If invited by friends from another religion, and it is deemed appropriate, Catholics may in exceptional circumstances attend their prayer-services or meditation. By doing this, and by our whole manner during the visit, we have the opportunity of showing respect for our hosts' religious traditions and for the texts they hold in reverence. By our prayerful composure and by praying in our hearts we are witnessing to the universal presence and action of the Holy Spirit. Good relations and bonds of friendship are fostered by this, and once again the Church is fulfilling her mission of being the sacrament of uniting people to God and to each other.

147. On the practical level, experience shows that it is wise to make arrangements well in advance, so as to agree on dates and times that are mutually convenient, and to enable everyone to prepare properly. Information should be obtained regarding appropriate dress and behaviour (and posture, if we are to be present at worship). Our attitude should be one of 'respectful presence' regarding the symbolic actions and objects of the community we are visiting.

148. *Giving Hospitality:* We must be aware of the religious sensitivities of our guests, and of course give a full and honest witness to our own faith and its liturgical expression. We should give guests any information that will help them to be at ease. They should be assured that they may wear their traditional dress, need not remove headgear or shoes, and need not take part in any singing, praying, standing or kneeling, unless they wish. They should be provided with clear copies of the service and, if possible, be seated with someone who can guide them through the service in a friendly way.[56]

149. The 'Multi-Faith Pilgrimage', in some places called the 'Walk for Friendship', is another way of both giving and receiving hospitality. On these walks, people of all religions and none walk together over a full day, visiting various places of worship. At each place a programme is arranged by the host-community, and at least once in the day there is a meal together. Bonds of friendship and understanding can be forged on these days, lasting beyond the pilgrimage day itself.

150. *Response to Events:* In situations of conflict, such as those in Iraq or Palestine, or after outrages such as the 2001 attack on the USA or the 2005 London bombings, people of different religions have felt the need to meet in order to pray. Another example, this time after a natural disaster, was the 2004 tsunami. Gatherings on occasions like these are a powerful witness to the oneness of our human family beyond the boundaries of the different traditions; they manifest love of our neighbour and our solidarity with them. We have already referred to the Holocaust Memorial Day each January, and the three meetings at Assisi, which in their different ways are all religious responses, instinctively wanting to pray in the face of the evils that threaten peace and concord.

Conclusion: The Spirit of Multi-Religious Prayer

151. A common mark of all such occasions must be the respect shown to the religious identity of each of the participants while they are witnessing to the religious traditions they come from. We must never treat these services as mere spectacle to indulge our curiosity or worst of all as occasions for rivalry. Those taking part should not feel that by so doing they are accepting everything that is said, or that they are

---

[56] Cf. Bishops' Committee for Other Faiths, *Prayer and Presence, Guidelines on inviting members of Other Faiths to Celebrations in Catholic Churches*, 2004.

showing a relativist attitude: 'Respect' is something shown to the person who believes and testifies – it is not the same as agreeing with the whole of his/her testimony.

152. It is much to be recommended that the form of such multi-religious prayer follow that used at Assisi. No prayer is voiced in common, and the integrity of each tradition is respected. Extreme care must be taken to avoid syncretism (smoothing over vital differences). The right sense of unity can be created by symbolic gestures, such as asking people from the different traditions each to light a candle from a lit candelabrum, or taking part in a common fast, or simply sitting together in silent meditation. Such gestures have proved to be very powerful. But the mere gesture of coming together in one place, the symbol of 'the gathering' united in common humanity and common concern, is surely the most powerful gesture of all.

Chapter 5:
INTERRELIGIOUS MARRIAGE

153. In Britain today, Catholics do not only marry those of other Christian traditions and those of no faith-adherence, but also those from other religions. The Second Vatican Council, later documents of the Holy See, the Code of Canon Law and guidance by Bishops' Conferences have all given indications on how to proceed.[57]

The Christian Perception of Marriage

154. The pastoral support and formation of Catholics contemplating an interreligious marriage need to be based on Catholic teaching regarding (a) marriage as such, as the Creator intended it; and (b) marriage between baptised Christians, as Christ has sacramentally raised it. The Church's canon law is based on that teaching.

155. *Marriage in General:* Marriage, as the life-long monogamous union of man and woman, is part of our Creator's intention and blessed by him from the beginning (Cf. *Gn* 1-2). All marriages have as their purpose and essential nature: (i) A life-long and exclusive union of two spouses in love, ordered towards their common good; and (ii) An orientation to the birth and upbringing of children:

> *The marital union of man and woman, which is founded and endowed with its own proper laws by the Creator, is by its very nature ordered to the communion and good of the couple and to the generation and education of children. According to the original divine plan this conjugal union is indissoluble, as Jesus*

---

[57] Cf. Vatican II, Pastoral Constitution On the Church In the Modern World *Gaudium et Spes* (*Joy and Hope*) 1965, 47-52; John Paul II, Apostolic Exhortation *Familiaris Consortio* (*On the Christian family*) 1981; *Code of Canon Law* 1983, cc.1055-1165; Joint document of the Pontifical Council for Interreligious Dialogue and the World Council of Churches on Mixed Marriages, 1997, etc.

Christ affirmed: 'What God has joined together, let no man put asunder' (Mk 10:9).[58]

156. Christian Marriage, that is when both bride and bridegroom are baptised, has been raised by Christ to the dignity of a sacrament, giving the couple a special grace to live their marriage as a sign of Christ's faithful love for the Church: *Husbands, love your wives as Christ loved the Church* (Ep 5:25). The Christian family is often referred to as the 'domestic church', because it is called to live out and symbolise the nature of the Church as the beloved family of God:

The Christian family is called the domestic church because the family manifests and lives out the communal and familial nature of the Church as the family of God. Each family member, in accord with their own role, exercises the baptismal priesthood and contributes towards making the family a community of grace and of prayer, a school of human and Christian virtue and the place where the faith is first proclaimed to children.[59]

157. Marriage in Other Religious Traditions: We acknowledge the commitment to marriage and the family shown by other religious traditions. Marriage and family life are at the heart of their cultures. Families in other traditions such as Hindu, Jewish, Muslim or Sikh are founded on their traditional religious and moral values, and like Christian families they feel threatened by the permissiveness of the prevailing ethos today. Indeed the importance they give to marriage and the family manifests once again the unity of the human race at its creation and in its common aspirations. We should collaborate with these religions, as much as in conscience we are able, in witnessing to the dignity and crucial importance of marriage in contemporary British society.

158. The Problems facing Interreligious Marriages: Nevertheless, we must also say that interreligious marriages, because of the great differences between religions and often also between cultures, can give rise to serious problems. For example, the situation of women in

---

[58] *Compendium of the Catechism of the Catholic Church*, no.338.

[59] *Compendium*, no.350.

some interreligious marriages can be extremely difficult for women who have grown up in a different culture.

159. *Support for those intending an Interreligious Marriage:* Once an interreligious couple have decided to marry, however, they are entitled to every support. Catholic support should of course be based on the Church's understanding of marriage, but it also needs to be based on the Church's teaching on Other Religions as it has developed since the Second Vatican Council. Consequently, the beliefs and religious practices of the partner who is not Christian must be treated with proper respect, and given every possible consideration consistent with Catholic faith and teaching. Part of the goodness of any legitimate marriage is that it is blessed by, and comes from, the one God whose will it is to bring every human being to salvation.

160. In spite of the serious difficulties that can arise, there are certainly fine examples of such marriages. An interreligious marriage can offer opportunities for deepening faith and for cultural enrichment. It is in such marriages that dialogue between people of faith can be at its most profound: a 'Dialogue of Life'. If such a marriage is to flourish, such dialogue is a necessity.

161. The couple's families and friends, and their religious communities, have an essential role in supporting them and in encouraging them to live out the values they have in common, as well as the values of their own tradition. At all costs the people with most influence in their lives must not use one religion competitively against the other. Their aim and their prayer must be that religion become a source of enrichment in their marriage, not a burden and a cause of conflict.

The Law of the Church

162. The *Code of Canon Law* (*CIC*) sets out specific regulations for Catholics who want to marry unbaptised persons. This is a situation described technically in the law as 'disparity of cult'.[60] Because of the

---

[60] This is different from the situation when a Catholic marries a baptised Christian from another tradition (e.g. the Church of England). Church law calls this 'mixed marriage'.

great variety of circumstances in which people wish to marry, the law requires that those in the situation of 'disparity of cult' must be granted a dispensation by the local bishop for the marriage to be 'valid' (i.e. for it to be a marriage at all). This dispensation can only be granted if the following conditions are met[61]:

(i) The Catholic partner must declare that he/she is prepared to remove any danger of defecting from the faith, and must promise sincerely to do all in their power within the unity of the marriage to ensure that all the children are baptised and brought up in the Catholic faith;

(ii) The partner from another religion must be informed in good time of the promises the Catholic has to make, so that he/she is certainly aware of the promises;

(iii) Both partners are to be instructed about the purpose and essential nature of marriage, which the Catholic Church teaches as being of divine law, not merely human law. This 'essential nature' is that it be a monogamous, life-long and faithful union, freely entered into by a man and a woman, and open in principle to the conception and rearing of children. The acceptance of this understanding of marriage must not be excluded by either partner, because it is essential to the validity of the marriage.

Marriage Preparation

163. Everyone involved closely in an interreligious marriage (the couple, their families, their advisers) need to ponder its implications very seriously. The wedding celebration itself is obviously a matter the partners and their families will need to consider very carefully, but far more important is the way the couple will live their life afterwards, including of course their religious life. The time of preparation before marriage is of the utmost importance, and the couple should be given every encouragement to recognise the challenges ahead, and to reach agreement between themselves on how they are going to meet them.

---

[61] Cf. *CIC*, c.1125.

Those who counsel them have a vital role here, especially concerning how they are each going to practise their own religion. They must certainly consider the following:

(i) They need to agree on the upbringing and religious education of their children, well before committing themselves to marriage;

(ii) They should think about how they are going to deal with any pressure to convert to the other religion, or at least to restrict them in the practice of their own. This pressure could come from the other partner, or his/her family, or from their wider religious community;

(iii) As mentioned earlier, there must be a full and honest explanation of the Catholic teaching on marriage, and of the obligations of the Catholic partner. The same applies to an explanation of the beliefs and obligations of the partner of another religion, and especially an explanation of the meaning of marriage for him/her and for the tradition they belong to;

(iv) The local bishop or his representative will have to be approached, with a request for a dispensation from the impediment of 'disparity of cult', giving the reasons for the request. For this, expert advice and help needs to be sought from Church authorities. The parish priest, or his representative with responsibility for the marriage preparation, will assist with obtaining this advice.

164. Although expert advice may be necessary, there are in any case many others closer at hand to give support and guidance. There is the parish priest, and there is often a team in the parish which has marriage preparation and support as its special ministry. Every diocese has a trained group of marriage counsellors. In addition, a most valuable form of support, if available, can be that of other interreligious families.

165. As far as priests and deacons are concerned, it is obvious that the pastoral care they provide will be greatly enhanced if in their initial training, and in on-going pastoral formation, they have become well-

informed about other religions, and about the Catholic Church's teaching on interreligious dialogue and relations.

166. Anyone, priest or otherwise, involved in this ministry will have to bear the following in mind:

(i) A genuine respect must be shown for the other partner's religion, but at the same time the Catholic's religious identity must be carefully affirmed and supported. Both partners should be given every opportunity to explain and discuss their personal understanding of their own faith and its commitments;

(ii) Young couples in this situation can face strong opposition from their relatives and friends. This may make them feel very isolated, and can drive them (either by revolt or acquiescence) into making decisions they are not yet mature enough to honour. They should be helped to be open and honest with one another, open to God in prayer, and honest with themselves as they contemplate the future;

(iii) *The Wedding itself:* Very often the parents of the couple find the whole prospect of an interreligious marriage a traumatic experience. The priest responsible can help to adapt the ceremony within canonical and liturgical limits, for instance by using appropriate symbols, in order to respect the sensitivies of both families.[62]

(iv) *After the Wedding:* Those who have had pastoral care of the couple need to be willingly available and supportive to everyone concerned as the newly-married couple set out on their married

---

[62] A wedding involving a Catholic must normally take place in the presence of a priest or deacon, and two witnesses. This stipulation is called 'canonical form'. It is presumed that it takes place in a Catholic church. For very exceptional reasons, the Bishop or his representative may dispense the couple from some or even all of these conditions. For instance, in exceptional circumstances he may permit the wedding to take place in a 'neutral' venue, or even in a non-Christian place of worship, and be conducted by a non-Christian official. When this is allowed it is absolutely essential that the couple freely exchange their consent at the same time as each other and to the same official, that their consent be to the purpose and nature of marriage as the Church understands it, and that it be properly witnessed. (Cf. *CIC* cc.1108, 1118, 1127-29).

life. Indeed, couples of different religions arguably need more than ordinary pastoral care. For example, the Catholic partner must not be treated as an oddity by the Catholic community, and likewise the community of the other partner must not feel they are losing one of their members. Such families therefore call for special care, both by the parish and, where applicable, by the Catholic school.

Chapter 6:
AT THE LOCAL LEVEL

We turn finally to the scene we are all most familiar with: our dioceses, our neighbourhoods and parishes, our schools and the places where we work.

The Situation today: Uneven Distribution of Population

167. Our Catholic dioceses differ considerably in the number of people they contain who belong to other religions, and in how the latter compare numerically with the rest of the population. The dioceses that serve the larger conurbations contain a higher proportion of other believers, because these tend to live in the larger urban areas, yet it is safe to say that there is no diocese in England and Wales where other religions are entirely absent. Even in dioceses with a greater number, the communities normally cluster in certain localities, so that Catholic parishes will have very varied experiences, and different opportunities for dialogue.[63] Again, the Catholic population itself is not evenly spread across the country, and varies markedly from one diocese to another. This will obviously have a bearing on the opportunities a diocese has to meet and relate with those of other religions.

168. In other words, there is great variation across the Church in England and Wales, and this will inevitably affect interreligious activity. Yet we must not exaggerate the differences. There is one 'national context' which, though changing all the time, presents opportunities which we will describe.

The religions and Civil Authorities

169. *Changes in Government Attitudes:* Our society is a complex one. Governments have their own agendas and their own procedures,

---

[63] Of course, whatever the state of affairs in the parish, other religions may well be present in parishioners' places of work, or where they go to school.

which do not always harmonise with those of religious communities, Christian or otherwise. For example, governments can tend to ignore differences between religions. This can, among other things, have the effect that the special position of Christianity in this country is overlooked, or the specific beliefs of the Catholic Church within Christianity. Generalisations are therefore unhelpful. Nevertheless, within government recently there has been a greater tendency to see what they call 'faith-communities' as partners in the search for social cohesion, rather than as obstacles to it; and it is of course the case that these religious communities can, in ways consistent with their own customs, help in the delivery of services, especially in the more deprived areas. Where this is happening, we as Catholics can see this as an excellent opportunity for the 'Dialogue of Action' described earlier, in which the followers of different religions work together for the common good.

170. This change in government thinking comes from the welcome realisation that religious communities are an extremely important part of civil society, with a contribution no other group can provide.[64] To begin with, they have the resource of a large number of religiously motivated *volunteers*, who will respond instinctively to others in need: to mothers and young children, to young people, to the elderly, and to vulnerable members of society. Through these volunteers the religions are in daily touch with some of the most deprived and most inaccessible of our citizens, who so often live in places most threatened by social tensions.

171. This new awareness is not peculiar to Britain. Governments elsewhere are realising how valuable the religions can be in reaching the most needy.[65]

---

[64] See *Faith and Community: a good practice Guide for Local Authorities* (Local Government Association 2002); and *Working Together: Co-operation between Government and Faith Communities* (Home Office 2004).

[65] Speaking on 11th January 2007, Jim Murphy, Minister for Employment and Welfare Reform, said on a visit to East London: *In Australia for example the Salvation Army, Mission Australia and Centrecare all have a long history of involvement in welfare delivery, helping those people who traditionally have shied away from the state. I see no reason why the same cannot happen here. (www.dwp.gov.uk/mediacentre /pressrelease/2007/jan/drc010-110107.asp)*

172. A religion's buildings form another part of the 'social capital' or resource for greater cohesion. Religious buildings, though often prominent, tend to be undervalued as a social asset. Yet they are the venue of choice for many local community activities, and in emergencies such as the floods of 2007 they provided shelter and support.[66] This can be an aid, not only to social cohesion, but also to the 'Dialogue of Action'. These buildings are sometimes a severe drain on a community's finances, but they can be a valuable resource for promoting good relations between members of different races and religions. They also happen often enough to be a significant part of the nation's cultural heritage.

173. Now that the authorities are more alert to this potential within the religions, their official guidelines will often stress the importance of consulting religious communities on matters of public policy, and will sometimes even allocate resources to enable religions to cooperate with them more effectively.

174. Authorities know the value of liaising with the leaders of religious communities. Religious leaders are their indispensable allies in the search for social cohesion, because by their example of friendship and dialogue with other religious traditions they can encourage their communities to do the same. Because Christianity is the majority religion, it is Christian leaders in particular who have a crucial role as 'bridge-builders'. Public authorities recognise this.

175. *'Local Strategic Partnerships':* The willingness of government to work with religious communities must be understood within their desire for a wider 'stakeholder' engagement, so that more groups feel

---

[66] On 18th June 2008, two documents published by the Faith Communities Team at the Department for Communities and Local Government drew substantially on good practice within the Catholic community: (1) *Key Communities, Key Resources: Engaging the Capacity and Capabilities of Faith Communities in Civil Resilience.* This document is intended to help emergency planners and faith communities through that process. It deals with principles and provides tools and a 'road map' for good practice (*http://www.communities.gov.uk/publications/communities/civilresilience*); (2) *Faith Communities and Pandemic Flu: Guidance for Faith Communities and Local Influenza Pandemic Committees.* This booklet explains how faith communities can play a part in protecting themselves and others in the event of a UK influenza pandemic (*http://www.communities.gov.uk/publications/communities/influenzapandemic*).

that they have a 'stake' in society and are not alienated from it. 'Local Strategic Partnerships' are an attempt by local authorities to bring together in partnership various parts of the public and private sectors, in order to address issues that matter to local people, and to ensure that public funding is effectively targeted. The hope is that in this way public sector concerns such as education, health, social services and the police will work better between themselves but also alongside community, voluntary and religious organisations, in order to find ways of improving public services. No one partner, not even local government, has all the answers; recognising this, they know that religious communities, as we have noted, can at times mobilise large numbers of volunteers who are sometimes the only routes to the most vulnerable, and the hardest to reach.

176. We strongly encourage Catholics, both as individuals and in our Catholic societies and agencies, to respond as much as they can to these government invitations and be willing to work in partnership with statutory bodies, with people, communities and organisations of other religions, and indeed with anyone involved in these projects. It goes without saying that all Catholic cooperation in these matters has to be true to Catholic principles and values. In fact Catholics should encourage discussion and debate on the values implicit in public policy, because there is a dialogue to be had here in which all religious communities will have a significant contribution to make. Prompt and constructive response by Catholics to government-initiated consultation-exercises inevitably strengthens the effectiveness of Catholic intervention on other aspects of public policy.

177. A further by-product of this collaboration between the religious communities themselves and the public bodies must surely be dialogue and collaboration between the communities themselves. So we repeat that the government's invitation to come and work alongside them is a golden opportunity for Catholics and other Christians to engage in a real 'Dialogue of Action' with our fellow-citizens from other religions over matters which concern us all.

178. *The Role of the Laity:* Much of this activity is specifically one for the laity to be engaged in, as Vatican II pointed out:

All that makes up the temporal order: the means of livelihood and family life, culture, the economy, the arts and professions, the institutions of the political community, international relations... are not only helps to the final end of human beings but have their own value given them by God...

Lay people should take the restoration of the temporal order as their proper function, and work directly at this in their specific manner, led by the light of the gospel and the mind of the Church and motivated by Christian charity...[67]

The Practice of Dialogue in the Diocese and the Parish

179. The encouragement that civil authorities are now giving to the religions to work with them and with each other for the common good is also an encouragement to seek interreligious dialogue in diocese and parish. Catholics are becoming more aware of the need of this, though there is often uncertainty about how to do it. In England and Wales we Catholics are relative newcomers to this work of the Lord. Traditionally Catholics have tended to view those of other religions exclusively as people in need of conversion; it takes quite a journey of mind and heart to respond to the Church when it calls us to dialogue with those we were previously only exhorted to call to Christ and welcome into the fold.

180. Young people, for the most part, tend to have fewer inhibitions, and some dioceses are seeking ways of linking their Youth Services with the work of interreligious dialogue.[68]

181. The activities already happening are varied and imaginative.[69] They are still dependent on the dedication of a few, as is so often the case with new ventures, so we pray that *Those who are sowing in tears will sing when they reap* (Ps 125:5). It is heartening to see this response

---

[67] Vatican II, Decree On the Apostolate of the Laity *Apostolicam Actuositatem* (*Apostolic Activity*), 1965, 7.

[68] The first national Catholic Youth Interfaith Forum took place in 2007, after a workshop at the National Youth Conference in Birmingham.

[69] For some examples see Appendix I

to the call of the Lord. We bishops want to state clearly that this spirit of dialogue and mission needs to spread, and it is our task as your pastors, charged as we are with the task of evangelisation, to foster this spirit with our encouragement, our careful discernment and our help.

182. We have become increasingly aware of the urgent need of interreligious dialogue as part of the Church's evangelising mission, though we cannot forget what we said at the beginning of this Document that clergy and people already have heavy demands on their time and energy. Nevertheless we must respond to the Lord's call, and to this end (depending on the needs and resources of a particular diocese) we have been taking initiatives such as appointing Interreligious Coordinators and other personnel, with whatever structures are appropriate, to support those who work in this mission.

183. Of particular importance is the formation that takes place. This must be of high quality, and thoroughly in accord with the Catholic Church's developed teaching on interreligious dialogue. The catechetical and adult educational structures of our dioceses are well placed to provide the theological and spiritual groundwork for this, and we would urge those involved in these structures to develop this side of their work even more. Both clergy and laity need to feel secure in the knowledge that involvement in interreligious relations is part of our baptismal calling. However, this calling respects the individuality of each of us; we are not all called to be involved in the same way or to the same degree.

184. *Diocesan Coordinators:* Diocesan Interreligious Coordinators now have a national network, supported by the Bishops' Committee for Other Faiths. This enables them to learn from each other's experience. A two-way strategy is gradually developing: there is an 'inward' focus, leading to programmes of formation for clergy and laity, so that everyone can learn about other religions, and understand the nature of dialogue and its part in the Church's mission; and there is an 'outward' thrust, leading to contacts and constructive relations with the believers of other religions – in other words, to dialogue in all its forms.

185. The work of the Diocesan Coordinator and the Diocesan Interreligious Commission will naturally overlap with the work of all in the diocese involved in justice and peace issues, for example the Justice and Peace Commission, those who come to the aid of asylum-seekers and refugees, and those who help ex-prisoners.

186. *Councils of Faiths:* Catholics entering the field of interreligious relations will be heartened to find that they are not walking alone. Most local authorities now have what are variously called a 'Council of Faiths' or an 'Inter-Faith Forum'. The Welsh Assembly government has established an 'All Wales Inter-Faith Forum'. The government publication *Face to Face and Side by Side: a Framework for inter-faith Dialogue and social Action*[70] reflects in its title the spectrum of approaches these groups represent. Making use of a phrase first used by the Chief Rabbi, Sir Jonathan Sacks, 'Face to Face' refers to interreligious dialogue between people of faith, while 'Side by Side' describes the joint activity of people from different traditions when they together undertake social activity in the wider community, or collectively engage with statutory bodies over matters of public policy.

187. It is sometimes quite a challenge for these councils to make a start and to run smoothly, but they have a validity and status that enables the local authority to engage seriously with them. The membership is worked out so that all religious traditions are involved and no single group predominates. Such councils require, and often urgently need, Catholic participation, preferably when the diocese is in a position to nominate its representatives officially. Public officials tend to assume that only the ordained clergy can take part in decision-making on behalf of the Catholic community; but if the bishop nominates a lay person to attend meetings with strategic decision–makers it should be made clear that the Catholic nominee is fully mandated to negotiate with the other partners.

188. *Other Interreligious Groups:* There are many other more informal interreligious bodies across the country, often pre-dating the Councils of Faiths.[71] These more informal groupings have usually been

---

[70] Department for Communities and Local Government, December 2007.

[71] See *Inter-Faith Organisations in the U.K: a Directory*, 4th edn. 2007, the Directory for the Inter-Faith Network for the U.K. (*www.interfaith.org.uk/publications/index.htm*).

created by the religious communities themselves in order to improve mutual understanding, and their membership is normally open to all interested parties. Our fellow-Christians are well represented on these, and Catholics are gradually beginning to play their part. They have programmes of meetings and discussions, arrange visits to one another's places of worship, and share food. Some groups conduct interreligious prayer on the 'Assisi' model, in which they come together to pray, but not to pray together. In one diocese, for example, two religious sisters (of Mercy and of St Louis) have worked with a Columban priest, other Catholics and local Christians to provide weekly ecumenical Christian prayer to support interreligious work, and on the 11th of every month a Christian group associated with them facilitates multi-religious prayers for peace at a local Council of Mosques community centre.

189. *The Value of an Ecumenical Approach:* It is of course perfectly appropriate for the Catholic community to take its own initiatives in these matters, as other Christians do, but we do stress that interreligious relations are often conducted more effectively when we do so as Christians together. Pope Benedict has emphasised that one important reason for Christian unity is the impetus it can give to interreligious dialogue, so that we can go out to other religions as one in Christ.

190. *The Roles of Clergy and Laity:* It is obviously true that some clergy have a particular gift for the work and an interest in it, and some will be appointed and specially trained for it; but in the nature of the case it is usually the laity who are best placed for dialogue, especially the 'Dialogue of Life' and the 'Dialogue of Action'. The parish priest's principal task is to give leadership by making it clear that interreligious dialogue accords with the teaching of the Church; by giving his interest and support, and where appropriate his advice and constructive criticism, to any interreligious activity taking place; by giving spiritual backing through the parish worship (e.g. in the Prayers of the Faithful) and through encouraging the prayers of the parishioners; and by giving his cooperation to those who are managing programmes of formation. In other words, as the ordained leader of the community it is the priest's task to enable and encourage the laity to fulfil theirs.

191. *Programmes of Formation:* In places where this is not already happening, those responsible for parish and school formation should think of including the Catholic Church's teaching on interreligious dialogue in their syllabus, geared of course to the people concerned. Diocesan Coordinators are often involved in setting up programmes tailored to parish needs, usually related to diocesan schemes of adult formation. We strongly urge the diocesan organisers of the Catholic Certificate in Religious Studies to include a module on the theology, spirituality and practice of interreligious dialogue.

192. *The Contribution of the Religious Orders:* We want to acknowledge in a very special way the contribution of the religious orders and congregations, and other institutes of consecrated life, both female and male, to every form of dialogue and the better understanding of other religions. The Society of Jesus, for instance, with its long history of missionary and academic experience, has a rich tradition here and abroad of theological study of other religions and of dialogue with them. Some monastic and contemplative orders engage in dialogue with followers of the contemplative and mystical traditions in Hinduism, Buddhism and the Sufi tradition of Islam, and with the monastic life in Buddhism.

193. The missionary congregations, with their extensive experience of the religions of the countries they have served in, are now often to be found at work in our parishes. They frequently have unrivalled access into the families and communities of other religions; they are often fluent in their language, and build up a friendship and trust that has increased over the years. They frequently link their apostolate to the general mission of the Church among disadvantaged families, and among those seeking asylum and refugee status. In particular we want to express our appreciation of the work of religious sisters in this field.

194. In relation to the Jewish people, the Sisters of Our Lady of Sion have borne a quite exceptional witness. They have always been aware of the relationship between Christianity and Judaism, but from the time of the Shoah (the Holocaust), and especially since *Nostra Aetate*, they have been deeply conscious of God's faithful love for the Jewish people. They dedicate themselves to the promotion of dialogue and of a fuller appreciation of Judaism and the relationship between our two faiths.

195. *Greetings from the Holy See:* The Pontifical Council for Interreligious Dialogue has the custom of sending greetings to Muslims at the time of Eid, to Hindus at Diwali, and to Buddhists at Vesakh. The local bishop has often added his own personal message. These greetings are much appreciated by the communities that receive them. There is no reason, of course, if the bishop deems it to be appropriate, why local greetings should not also be sent to the Jewish community (e.g. at Passover), or to the Sikhs perhaps at the Birth of Guru Nanak. Indeed, the parish priest could in some places add a word of greeting from his parish community, and send it to the local mosque, synagogue or temple. Such simple gestures certainly help to break down barriers.

Catholic Schools and Other Religions

196. There is much debate in society today about the value and purpose of schools that are set up by faith communities. Some see them as divisive or elitist and would seek to close them down. Some view their religious curriculum as narrow and would seek to broaden what is offered. Others value them and appreciate what is offered within them, seeking a faith education for their children even if they are not part of the particular religion that runs that school. We, the bishops of England and Wales, view our Catholic schools as an essential part of our mission not only in relation to the Catholic population but also in regard to how Catholics relate to people of other religions.

197. In September 2007, we published a Pastoral Letter on Catholic Schools which highlighted our re-affirmation of our vision of Catholic education and our commitment to providing Catholic schools. We also highlighted how successful our schools are and the contribution they make to society in general.

198. At the same time, the government issued a significant statement expressing unequivocal support for schools of a religious character as a vital part of the provision of education in England (and Wales). The statement, entitled *Faith in the System*, was published with the full agreement of the providers of schools of a religious character.

199. Both the Pastoral Letter and *Faith in the System*, as well as earlier Church documents, recognise that our Catholic schools are not necessarily made up entirely of Catholics. In fact, the nature of our schools varies enormously and parents from other religious communities often seek and are granted places within them for their children. Whatever the make up of a particular school, we believe it has a role to play in interreligious dialogue both within the school itself and within the wider community where the school is situated.

200. It is perhaps helpful to return here to the definitions of interreligious dialogue that we gave earlier in this document (nn.1-4). In-depth conversations about spiritual, theological or scholarly matters may find a place in more advanced courses of study within the religious education curriculum but this would not normally be the starting point for interreligious dialogue in our schools.

201. Pope John Paul II's definition of such dialogue as *a way of living in positive relationship with others* is the best starting point. Within our schools we are seeking to educate all pupils of whatever religion to be able to live a way of life that integrates their beliefs with all other aspects of what it means to be human. As part of this, they must learn to live alongside others who are different and hold alternative views, including religious views.

202. In September 2008, the Bishops' Conference Department for Catholic Education and Formation issued some very specific guidance to schools about how they might develop this approach within their pupils. Entitled *Catholic Schools, Children of Other Faiths and Community Cohesion: Cherishing Education for Human Growth*, the document took as its basis a concept put forward by Pope John Paul II and affirmed by Pope Benedict XVI. This was the 'ecology of human growth', suggesting that the school can create a climate in which pupils can grow and develop in accordance with the environment in which God has placed them.

203. In fact, this 'ecology of human growth' consists of a number of interlocking 'ecologies' and each of these ecologies can also be described as a particular type of dialogue. The document describes three such ecologies: the ecology of daily living (loving tenderly), the ecology of justice (acting justly), the ecology of faith and religious experience (walking humbly).

204. This model of the ecology corresponds well with another description in interreligious dialogue given earlier – developing a frame of mind so that people are happy to simply live as good neighbours (n.3).

205. That definition also includes the idea of learning more specific things about particular religions and about how their members live. This approach is reflected in the religious education curriculum offered in our schools, in the schemes of work and in its assessment. Broadly speaking it is described by the joint approach of 'learning about' and 'learning from' religion. Pupils are encouraged not simply to learn facts about other religions but also to reflect upon them and gain insights from them. That, in itself, is a valuable form of dialogue.

206. Finally, in terms of our definitions, there is the 1984 statement of the then Secretariat for non-Christians that dialogue *also includes all positive and constructive interreligious relations with individuals and communities of other faiths which are directed at mutual understanding and enrichment* (n.1). This finds particular resonance with all that our schools are doing to build up and contribute to community cohesion and we encourage that to continue.

207. In conclusion, our schools have much to contribute to interreligious dialogue by the way in which they form pupils to live in a multi-religious society. The vast majority of Catholics will never enter into interreligious dialogue in a formal academic or theological sense but each and every Christian or person of another religion is called to enter into interreligious dialogue by virtue of the fact that we live in a world of many religions. Day by day we share a world with others who hold their religious views with the same conviction as we hold ours. Catholic schools can help us prepare for that lifetime of interreligious dialogue.

Chaplaincies

208. Nowadays chaplaincies are often staffed by both lay and ordained people, and are very often ecumenical and multi-religious in make-up. Multi-religious chaplaincy teams are found in port and airport chaplaincies, in the armed forces, in healthcare, in prisons and in universities. Each has its own distinguishing features.

209. Catholic chaplains are an essential part of the chaplaincy team. They play a vital role in uniting the team in a commitment to supporting those they serve at what are often critical times of their lives. Catholic chaplains are confident in carrying out their ministry, rooted as they are in the integrity of the Catholic tradition, while cooperating fully with their colleagues from other traditions.

210. We must be clear, however, that out of faithfulness to Catholic belief and principle the Catholic chaplain cannot accept a chaplaincy provision that offers the resources of one tradition only, or reduces it to a common 'spirituality' in disregard of differences of faith. This 'generic' model of chaplaincy, which seeks to flatten out differences and implies they are of minor importance, is firmly resisted by Catholic chaplains, as it is indeed by others.[72]

---

[72] For a brief description of individual chaplaincies in relation to other religions, see Appendix II.

CONCLUDING REFLECTIONS

Jesus said to the crowds, 'When you see a cloud rising in the west, you immediately say "It is going to rain", and so it happens. And when you see the south wind blowing, you say "There will be scorching heat", and it happens. You hypocrites! You know how to interpret the appearance of earth and sky, but why do you not know how to interpret the present time?' (Lk 12:54-56)

211. The prophets of the Old Testament were enlightened by God to see his will for them within the events of their own time, the divine meaning in what was happening all round them. In the passage above, Jesus is speaking as the messianic Prophet, the fulfilment of prophecy. He is warning his audience that their lack of faith has made them blind to the unique, indeed the ultimate meaning of his presence among them.

212. To discern something of the meaning and purposes of God within contemporary events and circumstances calls indeed for the wisdom which is the gift of the Holy Spirit; but it also calls for a living faith in the reality of God intimately present and active in all that exists. If we are to read the 'signs of the times' aright, we need the gift of faith to remember that we always 'stand on holy ground'. This faith contradicts the present culture, in which even for believers it is very easy to live our everyday lives as though God did not exist, or inhabited some distant, irrelevant region.

213. It is characteristic of the Catholic 'sacramental' vision of reality that it sees all events and situations in which we find ourselves as 'God-bearers', carrying the gift and call of God. Earlier spiritual writers spoke of the 'sacramental' nature of present experience, 'the sacrament of the present moment', because every passing moment, light or dark, is a vehicle and an invitation of God's love. We do indeed 'stand on holy ground', whether its going be rough or smooth.

214. As we reflect, in faith, on our present moment, it is hard not to see some outstanding features as 'signs of the times', however we might interpret them: the gross disparity of wealth and poverty in the world and the threat of global warming are two obvious examples. Another feature, however, is the recent immigration of communities from other religions into a Europe whose religion and culture have been so shaped in a particular manner by Christianity. These communities are entering Europe at a time when Europe's traditional faith has been in decline for many years, and where the sense of the active presence of God has been eroded.

215. If we read this as a 'sign of the times' carrying the gift and call of God, how do we read it? The teaching of the contemporary Catholic Church and of this teaching document suggests that we read it as a call to renew our commitment to Christ and the Gospel, to pray for a deeper faith in the living presence of God, and in the confidence of that faith and with Christ within us, to go out in humble and persevering dialogue to our brothers and sisters in the great religions of the world.

216. To turn away from even the attempt to dialogue is to despair of the power of God and of his risen Son to advance his own Kingdom of peace and love. It is to forget that the work of dialogue, as with all forms of evangelisation, is not our work at all, but his. We are merely his 'earthen vessels', whose limitations show that *the extraordinary power belongs to God, and does not come from us* (2 Co 4:7). Christ is calling us to trust unflinchingly in that power:

> *Now to him who by the power at work within us is able to accomplish abundantly far more than all we can ask or imagine, to him be glory in the Church and in Christ Jesus to all generations, for ever and ever. Amen (Ep 3:20-21).*

APPENDIX I: Some Examples of Dialogue from our Dioceses

Archdiocese of Birmingham

217. The diocese has been well represented in meetings between the leaders of the main religious groups in Birmingham. These meetings have been taking place since the 1970s. They took on a new lease of life after the 2001 attack on the United States, and evolved into a close-knit group which meets once a month. In 2007 the group published a collection of the Saturday columns each member had in turn contributed to the *Birmingham Mail*, together with more formal statements and articles. They have also promoted faith literacy programmes. Most importantly the Faith Leaders have cooperated with the University of Birmingham and a range of City bodies, such as the Chamber of Commerce, in a systematic study of the place of religious faith in a modern city. The overall title of this initiative is *Faith in the City*. The Faith Leaders also played a significant part in the development of a revised Religious Education syllabus for all local authority schools.

Diocese of East Anglia

218. A group was set up in 2006 with the aim of increasing knowledge of the Church's teaching on interreligious relations among Catholics. In 2008 the committee raised £2,500 in sponsorship, and hired the Global Ethics Exhibition from the Global Ethics Foundation. During April 2008 the Exhibition was displayed in Our Lady and the English Martyrs, Cambridge, in St John's Cathedral, Norwich, and (in conjunction with the Anglican community) in Peterborough Cathedral. The presence of the Exhibition was advertised in churches and schools, and over a hundred local opinion-formers were invited to receptions at the three venues. Feedback was very positive. One parishioner wrote: 'Our parish priest recommended that we visit this Exhibition and I am very glad he did or I should not have known of it. If only everyone would "do as they would be done by" and follow the advice of their own religion, how much better the world would be!'

Diocese of Hexham and Newcastle

219. Asylum-seekers of every religion and none find a warm welcome at 'Drop In' sessions in north-east England. Set up by the Asylum Seekers and Refugees Project, an initiative of the Hexham and Newcastle Diocesan Justice and Peace Coordinating Council, the Drop Ins offer refreshments, recreation, chat in shared languages, conversational English practice, and advice from visiting agencies. Catholic parishes provide the Drop In venues and volunteers. Such parishes are in truth heeding the Lord's words, *I was a stranger and you welcomed me* (*Mt* 25:35). Food collected by over forty parishes and small amounts of money are given to failed asylum-seekers who have no accommodation or financial support, but who cannot be deported because, for example, there is no safe route.

Diocese of Leeds

220. A Catholic secondary school in Keighley serving, alongside its own Catholic students, other Christian pupils and those from the local Muslim community, has set aside a room beside the chapel as a reflection-room. Plainly furnished, it stands open all day, and is available for those who wish to pray but prefer not to use the Catholic chapel. While this is of especial use to the Muslim members, it also provides a congenial atmosphere for some of the Christian pupils who are not Catholics. The school has a formal sixth-form link with a neighbouring school which has a predominantly Asian membership. All lessons in the sixth-form are jointly taught, and on both sites, so that the students cannot opt for a menu of courses that allows them to stay in their own school. The school produces a prayer-card every year with the school calendar on the reverse. The prayers on the card change every year, but always include a 'guest' prayer from a religion other than Christianity.

Diocese of Middlesbrough

221. Catholics in the town of Middlesbrough responded well when the Local Authority set up a Council of Faiths, suggesting that local churches should have more grassroots involvement in community affairs. A thirty-three member Council now represents the town's ten Christian denominations and other religions, covering fifty nationalities and over eighty places of worship. Each religion hosts an event during the year, open to all, explaining an aspect of their belief and practice. The Catholics have found that dialogue with other religions does not compromise but rather strengthens their own faith.

Diocese of Northampton

222. In Luton a group of Catholics works to encourage dialogue between people of different religions and cultures. Their aim is to foster a vision of human solidarity and development, and the integrity of creation, and to move from mere dialogue to practical action for peace and justice. Their activities include: a multi-religious steering group working on the project 'Making Luton a Fair Trade Town'; a 'Faith Woodland' scheme to make a 'sacred space ' in Maulden Woods accessible to all religions; and an annual 'Faith Walk' with visits to churches, mosques, gurdwaras and Hindu temples. All these initiatives provide a refreshing experience of encounter and hospitality.

Diocese of Plymouth

223. Members of other religions, particularly Hindus, Jews and Muslims, have generously and enthusiastically contributed to a series of Inset days for Catholic primary school teachers, with some school governors, in the south-west of England. Entitled 'Seeking Wholeness', these days have been very well received. Those who attended have reported a deeper knowledge of Catholic teaching, a greater understanding of other religions, and an increased awareness of the resources, including personnel, which can support classroom teaching. It is hoped that this enterprise will in the near future be extended to parishes and secondary schools.

Archdiocese of Southwark

224. The Southwark Interfaith Group is a network of those involved in local interfaith groups and those working with Local Authorities to promote interreligious contacts. It has become clear that Local

Authorities are not often particularly interested in the dialogue between members of different religions: their agenda is to promote cultural diversity and social cohesion, rather than dialogue. Some of the members are therefore members of their Local Authority Multi-Faith Forum which addresses the social needs of different faith communities and their engagement with the wider community. Other members are involved with local interfaith groups which meet to promote dialogue and understanding; and others are involved in interfaith action groups which promote justice and peace working with Asylum seekers in Medway and Dover.

225. Among its many other activities the Interfaith Group has circulated information about interfaith talks and gatherings, and it has promoted and supported interfaith walks around the diocese visiting different churches, temples and mosques. These have been very popular. The group has also set up a chain of distribution for the messages of greeting sent from the Pontifical Council for Interreligious Dialogue to the various faith communities to mark their feasts and festivals and has helped local Catholics to contact their local mosque or temple and given them support in delivering the greetings message. The greetings have also been used in Catholic Schools and Colleges to promote awareness of inter-religious dialogue among the students.

Archdiocese of Westminster

226. For the last twenty-three years Westminster Interfaith has organised the annual Multi-faith Day Pilgrimage for Peace. People of all religions and none come from all parts of the country. The walk takes place in a designated part of London, visiting places of worship on the way, where there is a welcome by the hosts and information given about the particular religion and its place of worship. There is question time, a time of silent prayer, a tour of the place and refreshments. Most people find the pilgrimage a truly religious experience. In all religious traditions pilgrimage is a symbol of human life, and for us it also marks the desire to bridge our differences and build a world of peace, justice and friendship.

Diocese of Wrexham

227. In the inter-faith movement in Wrexham there are various religions represented at meetings including Hindus, Muslims, Christians, and other groups. Each religion is very well accepted and there is less fear among participants. We spend time together in prayer. Whenever we meet, there is a positive feeling of mutual respect and trust. We are able to discuss topics that help to unite us and we share our thoughts and views. The groups include students and older people. People are open and at peace with each other. On one occasion when we were leaving a celebration, a member of the Muslim community said how happy he was to have met with us, since our presence meant much to him. We know we still have a long way to go but we feel that we are making good progress.

Conclusion

228. This is but a small sample of the ways in which the call to dialogue is being answered in our dioceses, parishes and schools. The effort to reach out in friendship to those of other religions is gradually becoming a familiar part of the mission of the local church.

APPENDIX II: Individual Chaplaincies

Airport Chaplaincy

229. Airports are the crossroads of contemporary civilisation. Millions of passengers pass through them, and thousands of people are employed by the travel industry. Airport chaplains serve both passengers and staff in circumstances which can vary from the routine to security and emergency situations. Many chaplaincies are multi-faith teams, with Catholic chaplains working alongside colleagues from a range of other Christian traditions and other religions. This teamwork is especially important in the current climate of increased tension surrounding issues of religious identity. Given the variety of backgrounds of passengers and staff, chaplains have to be responsive to a wide range of religious sensitivities. Catholic airport chaplains seek to serve all they meet, of whatever faith or none, in a manner that is faithful to the Gospel and the teaching of the Church.

Apostleship of the Sea (Stella Maris)

230. Seaports and the ships that visit them include seafarers from a wide range of nationalities and religious backgrounds, including Catholic and Orthodox Christians, Muslims and Hindus.[73] For these seafarers, problems often stem from their stressful and isolated lives as well as from their religious needs. Chaplaincy teams offer assurance and support, helping them to communicate with their families at home as well as providing material help.

231. The chaplaincy team's focus is on the whole person. This is the foundation for the practical help they give as well as for the spiritual needs they try to meet. This approach provides opportunities for sharing belief and faith at a time when loneliness can lead to personal questioning and insecurity.

---

[73] See Kahveci, E., *Port Based Welfare Services for Seafarers*, (Cardiff, Seafarers International Research Centre, 2007), p.39.

Armed Forces

232. The military chaplain provides a sacramental, spiritual, pastoral and educative ministry within a diverse military environment. The Royal Navy, Army and Royal Air Force train chaplains to a military competence that enables them to minister within their respective Service. A chaplain will serve in a new setting usually every two years in a community which is equally as transient. As non-combatants, chaplains accompany units into war, on operations and exercises, and as such they must be physically and medically fit. Another important area of chaplaincy is caring for the families of serving personnel in their particular needs. Chaplaincy is also carried out within the training environment, where the armed forces look to the chaplain to contribute to the delivery of the moral component of service life.

233. As well as serving Catholic personnel, the chaplain must facilitate the needs of Christians from other denominations, as well as those of other world religions, or of no religion at all. Indeed, the chaplain's understanding of other religions helps to move forward the cause of world peace. It is a chaplain's task to grasp fully and debate with others the meaning of 'The Golden Rule', a maxim found in different forms in all the major religions: *In everything, do to others as you would have them do to you* (*Mt* 7:12).

234. Chaplains are to minister to all ranks and rates in a shared life of service, and to that end must be highly motivated, well-trained missionaries who are willing to take risks. Military personnel are asked to serve their country; chaplains are called to serve *them*, often outside the structures which are normally called 'parochial', but always within the context of community.

Healthcare Chaplaincy

235. Catholic chaplains work within an ecumenical and interreligious context. As well as ministering to Catholic patients and staff they also serve people from other Christian traditions together with those from other religions. There are, however, specific religious boundaries which entail that some faith communities can only be ministered to by those of their own tradition. NHS chaplaincy recognises this, and NHS trusts need to take it into account.

236. There are arrangements for the Catholic Church and the NHS to work together so that the public are protected and that Catholic chaplains are effective. These arrangements require that the relationship between the wider faith community and all chaplains needs to be clearly articulated[74].

237. Patients and healthcare staff have different religious needs that must be respected, and Catholic chaplains belong to and are accountable to their Church as well as to the NHS. This dual appointment of Catholic chaplains ensures that both patients and staff receive appropriate support.

Prison Chaplaincy

238. Prison chaplains seek to fulfil their role in a spirit of religious inclusiveness and collaboration, and to meet the needs of prisoners and staff from all religions and none. Prison chaplains are often at the forefront of developments in interreligious relations, as they strive to create better understanding and respect for all persons of any religion.

239. Catholic prison chaplains recognise the need and importance of building authentic partnerships with chaplains of other Christian traditions and other religions. They do this by providing general pastoral care for all the people they meet in prison, as well as care specific to Catholic prisoners and staff. Catholic chaplains see their fellow chaplains as colleagues in the Prison Service and together they promote the dignity and value of every prisoner and staff member.

University Chaplaincy

240. Universities today are undergoing profound change as educational institutions and this has an impact on the nature and provision of Catholic chaplaincies. Increasingly students and staff are

---

[74] Cf. Catholic Bishops' Conference of England & Wales, Department for Christian Responsibility & Citizenship, Healthcare Reference Group, *Caring for the Catholic Patient – a Guide to Catholic Chaplaincy for NHS Managers and Trusts*, (Catholic Truth Society, 2007).

coming from a diversity of cultural and religious backgrounds, and chaplaincies are seen as places of consequence for developing understanding between the religions, with the chaplains themselves often at the forefront in building personal relationships across the religious differences.

241. Catholic chaplains minister alongside their fellow chaplains in ecumenical and multi-religious situations. Many participate in 'faith forums' and celebratory events. Catholic chaplains contribute to building chaplaincy teams that allow each member to express his or her own tradition. Interreligious activity is carried out on sound theological principles: that is, the aim is to deepen understanding, so that dialogue with members of other religions challenges and develops faith in one's own. In some chaplaincies understanding is promoted by means of interreligious projects based on common concerns such as care for the environment and building community.

Book List

Conciliar Documents

Second Vatican Council, Dogmatic Constitution on the Church, *Lumen Gentium*, 1964.

Second Vatican Council, Pastoral Constitution on the Church in the Modern World, *Gaudium et Spes*, 1965.

Second Vatican Council, Declaration on the Relation of the Church to Non-Christian Religions, *Nostra Aetate*, 1965.

Second Vatican Council, Decree on the Church's Missionary Activity, *Ad Gentes*, 1965.

Second Vatican Council, Declaration on Religious Liberty, *Dignitatis Humanae*, 1965.

Second Vatican Council, Decree on the Apostolate of Lay People, *Apostolicam Actuositatem*, 1965.

Papal Teaching

Pope Paul VI, Encyclical Letter, *Ecclesiam Suam*, 1964.

Pope Paul VI, Apostolic Exhortation, *Evangelii Nuntiandi*, 1975.

Pope John Paul II, Apostolic Exhortation, *Familiaris Consortio*, 1981.

Pope John Paul II, Encyclical Letter, *Redemptoris Missio*, 1990.

Pope John Paul II, Apostolic Letter, *Novo Millennio Ineunte*, 2001.

Pope Benedict XVI, Encyclical Letter, *Deus Caritas Est*, 2005.

Pope Benedict XVI, Encyclical Letter, *Spe Salvi*, 2007.

Documents of the Holy See

Code of Canon Law, 1983.

Catechism of the Catholic Church, 1994.

Congregation for the Doctrine of the Faith, Declaration *Dominus Iesus*, 2000.

Pontifical Council for Interreligious Dialogue (formerly Secretariat for non-Christians), *The attitude of the Church towards the followers of other religions: Reflections and Orientations on Dialogue and Mission*, 1984.

Pontifical Council for Interreligious Dialogue and the Congregation for Evangelisation of Peoples, *Dialogue and Proclamation: Reflections and Orientations on Interreligious Dialogue for the Proclamation of the Gospel of Jesus Christ*, 1991.

Pontifical Council for Promoting Christian Unity, *Directory for the Application of Principles and Norms on Ecumenism*, 1993.

Pontifical Council for Promoting Christian Unity, Commission for Religious Relations with the Jews, *We Remember: A Reflection on the Shoah*, 1998.

Pontifical Council for Culture and Pontifical Council for Interreligious Dialogue, *Jesus Christ, The Bearer of the Water of Life*, 2003.

Pontifical Council for Refugees & Itinerant People, *Erga Migrantes Caritas Christi*, 2004.

Catholic Jewish Relations, Documents from the Holy See, (Catholic Truth Society, 1999).

Bishops' Conference of England and Wales

Catholic Schools and Other Faiths – a consultation paper prepared for the Bishops' Conference, 1997.

Committee for Other Faiths, *Prayer and Presence, Guidelines on inviting members of Other Faiths to Celebrations in Catholic Churches*, 2004.

Catholic Education Service, *On the Way to Life: Promoting and Supporting Catholic Education in England and Wales* (2005).

Committee for Other Faiths (now the Committee for Relations with other Religions), *Interfaith Dialogue: The Teaching of the Catholic Church*, 2002.

Committee for Other Faiths (now the Committee for Relations with other Religions), *Getting to know People of other Faiths*, 1999 (A series of leaflets on interreligious dialogue, giving brief introductions to the beliefs and practices of other religions).

Department of Christian Responsibility & Citizenship, Healthcare Reference Group, *Caring for the Catholic Patient – a Guide to Catholic Chaplaincy for NHS Managers and Trusts*, 2007.

Department for Catholic Education and Formation, *Catholic Schools, Children of Other Faiths and Community Cohesion: Cherishing Education for Human Growth*, September 2008.

Catholic Church and other Christians

Pontifical Council for Interreligious Dialogue and World Council of Churches, *Mixed Marriages*, 1997.

Mission and Public Affairs Council of the Church of England, *Presence and Engagement*, 2005.

Generous Love - an Anglican Theology of Inter-faith Relations, a Report from the Anglican Communion Network for Inter Faith Concerns, Anglican Consultative Council, 2008.

UK Government

Local Government Association, *Faith and Community: a good practice Guide for Local Authorities*, 2002.

UK Government Home Office, *Working Together: Co-operation between Government and Faith Communities*, 2004.

Department for Communities and Local Government, *"Face-to-Face and Side-by-Side": A framework for inter faith dialogue and social cohesion*, 2007.

Other Publications

Gioia, F., (ed.), *Interreligious Dialogue: the Official Teaching of the Catholic Church 1963-1995*, (Pauline Books, 1997).

Troll, Christian W., *Muslims Ask, Christians Answer* (Gujarat Sahitya Prakash, 2007).

Fitzgerald, M. L. and J. Borelli, *Interfaith Dialogue: A Catholic View* (SPCK, 2006).

Abbreviations used in the document

Ac – Acts of the Apostles

AG – *Ad Gentes* 'To the Nations'

2. *Apol.* – *Second Apology of St Justin Martyr*

Ch. – Chapter

CIC – *Code of Canon Law*

Col – Letter to the Colossians

Co – Letter to the Corinthians

DH – *Dignitatis Humanae* 'Human Dignity'

DI – *Dominus Iesus* 'Lord Jesus'

Ep – Letter to the Ephesians

Ga – Letter to the Galatians

Gn – Book of Genesis

Gioia – Gioia, F., (ed.), *Interreligious Dialogue: The Official Teaching of the Catholic Church 1963-1995*, (Pauline Books, 1997).

Jn – Gospel of John

Jude – Letter of Jude

LG – *Lumen Gentium* 'Light of the Nations'

Lk – Gospel of Luke

Mk – Gospel of Mark

Mt – Gospel of Matthew

n., nn. – paragraph(s)

NA – *Nostra Aetate* 'In our Age'

Ph – Letter to the Philippians

Ps – Book of Psalms

RM – *Redemptoris Missio* 'Mission of the Redeemer'

Rm – Letter to the Romans

UR – *Unitatis Redintegratio* 'Restoration of Unity'